Prospects:

How to Find 'Em,
Sign 'Em,
& What to Do
With Them
in Multilevel

Venus C. Andrecht

ACKNOWLEDGMENT

For my lovely, perceptive, and wise daughter,
Summer, who has counseled me almost from birth and now
edits, typesets, and designs my books while encouraging me to
leap ever deeper into the writing life.

Ransom Hill Press
PO Box 325
Ramona, CA 92065-0325
(800) 423-0620
Outside U.S. & Canada (760) 789-0620

Fourth Edition

ISBN 0-941903-13-3

TABLE OF CONTENTS

CHAPTER 1

PROSPECTING: WHERE TO BEGIN?

Let me begin with a little story: About fifteen years ago, I attended a new church and a strange lunch afterwards. The following incident sticks in my mind like a dagger tossed by a master knife thrower. I had been invited to the church by an acquaintance. "You'll really like it," she had said. "It's unique."

Well, that was true, and not the half of it. I'd met an interesting Canadian couple at the church named Henry and Clara. They were a skinny twosome, both in their seventies, and friendly as heck. They'd invited me to join them and several other people for lunch after the service.

Now, here we sat, waiting for our fried chicken and beans. I was a little shy, but since I was sitting next to Happy Henry, that didn't seem to matter. He appeared ready to bodily carry the conversation. As the group around us commenced to animatedly discuss the spiritual, Henry leaned close to me. His jaunty blue hat with the yellow feather played a duet with his blue polyester suit. He cleared his throat, tapped me on the arm, and launched into what was to be a startling conversation.

"I," he announced, "used to have *turrible* trouble with my balls." He paused and looked at me expectantly. I looked at his wife, Clara, horrified. How was I supposed to respond to this one? I didn't even know this old man, and I'd met him at church, for heaven's sake.

"Oh really?" I said politely.

"Yes!" Henry said. He slapped the table with his bony hand. "Turrible, turrible trouble with my balls. In fact, every few days they'd just bind up on me. Wouldn't move. Couldn't budge 'em."

Henry peered at me, his bushy brown eyebrows moving up and down. A graphic visual picture of his affliction passed before my eyes. *My* eyebrows went up and down.

"Oh really," I said again.

"I tell you," Henry intoned, rubbing his hands together, "life wasn't worth living. A problem like that affects your whole life. Everything I wanted to do was affected by my ball situation."

I glanced around the table. No one appeared interested in our conversation but us. And I was very interested. No one had ever told me about their ball problems before.

"It went on for years," Henry was saying. He looked at me intently. "You can imagine the embarrassing situations it caused me." He waited expectantly for my sympathy.

"Of course," I said weakly.

His voice now rose like a high wind behind a preacher exhorting his congregation for donations. "My ball troubles got in the way of all my relationships and even my work!" He let out a delirious whoop, smacked the table vigorously, and shouted, "And then! And then! I met a wonderful woman!"

"Clara?" I ventured, timorously.

"Donna!" he thundered. "It was *Donna* who cured my ball trouble!"

I gasped sharply and snapped around to stare at Clara. She smiled benignly, nodded *yes*, bent her gray head demurely, and took a sip of water.

"Really?!" I said.

"Yes!" Henry boomed. "That wonderful woman worked a miracle on my balls. She was a wonder."

Well, I guess she must have been! I stared at Henry. If two waiters carrying a roasted President of the United States, stuffed with pecans and raisins, had entered the dining room, it wouldn't have dislodged my attention from Henry. The old guy had me spellbound, mesmerized, and completely wrapped up in his conversation. He could have told me anything and sold me anything and signed me up for anything at this moment. And he did.

"That woman," Henry continued, "cured me with those herbs. Totally cured my bowel problems."

Bowel problems! Not *ball* problems! Henry's Canadian accent, I suddenly realized, had made *bowel* sound like *ball* to my untraveled ears!

I looked at Henry and began laughing. Henry laughed in return.

"Yes," he said, "I laughed, too, when I found that herbs got rid of my miserable situation. Everybody needs herbs!" He paused, then said semi-sincerely, "I can tell that you'd be really good at selling herbs to people. Listen, we're having a little get-together over at our house tonight. I want you to come, sweetie." He leaned closer. "You'll want to sign up with us. It's only $20 and you'll get all the herbs wholesale! And, there's money to be made here, I tell you. All you have to do is sign up people just like yourself."

Henry was right. I went to his get-together that night and I signed up. That was my first multilevel, and I was successful with it for a number of years.

My story about Henry is not only to shock, amaze, and horrify you, but to illustrate that there are all kinds of ways to prospect. Henry was prospecting me, and by golly, while his approach was laced with the unintended, he captured my attention completely. Sharp rocks dropping from the ceiling wouldn't have interrupted my focus on Henry and what he was saying. It never occurred to me that the man was prospecting me for his multilevel. And, even though he didn't realize that it wasn't his charm, knowledge, or compelling personality that kept me from running away from his multilevel attack, he still accomplished what he set out to do. He signed me. By the sheer uniqueness of his approach, unwittingly, he got me.

It's not usually that easy. Fifteen years later, I was out of multilevel and had been for five years. I had no intention of building one again. I wasn't as naive as I once had been, and I wasn't an easy prospect.

While prospecting, you'll meet plenty of people like me. Some will be jaded and sour about multilevel, or tired and worn out from it. Some will be afraid of multilevel, and some won't understand it. Others won't dare give it a chance for fear of looking stupid, and others will have utterly no interest. Many will yawn and tell you to scram, or they'll suddenly have to race to the bathroom in order to get away from you and your one-pointed conversation.

My Story

Let me tell you my story. After leaving my first multilevel, I became one of the tough ones to approach. I knew all the tricks and all the cunning maneuvers taught to and used by MLM solicitors. In spite of that, even though I said "No, no, no," eventually *someone* got me again, and I got *them* their retirement.

The last time I was vigorously prospected, I had become a regular person with a real job. I was also a divorced mother who was always worried about my lack of money and my future. I was just the kind of person who needed multilevel, but, like so many people, I didn't know it and didn't want to know it.

I was in desperate circumstances, but I lacked good sense. I say that because I had been told about a particular multilevel for a long time, but I actively ignored the hints about my future. Thankfully, however, Good Fortune kept her hand stretched out to me for at least two years. She influenced a number of people to call and come to see me with their company's product and brochures tucked neatly under their arms. "Here," someone would say, "just try this stuff. Read the literature. It could change your life."

I was charming and grinned a lot as I said, "Thank you so much," and promptly tossed my future into the trash. I wasn't quite dumb enough to get involved with another multilevel. I'd been in one years before, and in the end, because of my divorce, it hadn't turned out so well. Now people were pushing me and prodding me, trying to get me involved with them in some dopey plan with a scam company with a common product. I'd rather suffer and worry about making a living the regular way, I said. I was good at suffering and worrying. I knew how to do it.

Meanwhile, my financial life continued its slow slide, deeper into genteel poverty. I had a ten year old car, and for the first time in years, I was renting a home instead of owning one. I had no money for frivolous fun, and just enough in the bank to half cover one broken leg or similar occurrence. Still, like many of *your* prospects, I was closed to hearing about multilevel. What eventually woke me from my stupor was probably something a bit different than what will jog your people. *I* began hearing voices. One day an unusual thought dropped into my head. It said, "Go see Diane." Now, I hadn't seen or thought about my old friend Diane for over two years. Why was she suddenly flashing through my thoughts? We had worked together in my previous multilevel, the one which I had left far back in my past, along with old Henry and my ex-husband.

The Voice was insistent.

I went to see Diane. As I sat in her little shop, I had to marvel at her. She was filled with excitement, a spinning top of energy and good will. She had been involved for three weeks with "the most incredible multilevel anyone could imagine!" The same one, in fact, that I'd been hounded about for two years. As I sat, transfixed, I heard myself say, "I'll take a jug of that stuff you're selling." I didn't want a jug, but the request had shot out of my mouth, unintended and unqualified. Before I could snatch the words back, the Voice popped a bell-ringing thought into my noggin: "She's going to make retail money off you!" Reflexively, I shouted, "I'll sign up!" Perplexed, I wondered why I'd sign up to get a discount on a product that I didn't want, had no intention of drinking, and certainly would never sell. Diane told me later that she and her husband had danced wildly around the room for ten minutes after I left. They thought they had a hot one, can you imagine?

The outcome is that I, the reluctant prospect, after five years, finally saw the Multilevel Light again. After finding that the product worked, I proceeded to make $100,000 with my company in my first ten months. Now, six years later, I make a very comfortable five figure income each month, and I do it with multilevel, off my kitchen table. After being out of multilevel so long, it took me three months to figure out how to sign up a prospect again, but now I find that signing people is one of my fortes. In this tape and booklet, I'll happily share my people finding, signing, and "what to do with 'em" secrets with you.

The Right Mind Set — Don't Be Too Hungry

I grew up in a real estate family. Something my mother said about real estate customers that applies equally well to prospecting folks for your multilevel still sticks in my mind: Mom said, "People can always tell when you're hungry." In other words, when you're desperate for customers, clients, prospects, or whomever, people run from you like their pants are on fire.

The first thing you need to do in order to find the right people for your business is to change the way your mind may be working. If you're feeling desperate and hungry for good distributors, you may have to continue to live a low-rent life and eat peanut butter sandwiches while you interview your mind and inner self. The first thing you may need to do is work at finding and keeping a charitable heart. Practice pulling any petty jealousies and narrow thoughts you might have about people out by the tap root. We all have these disgusting thoughts and feelings, but those little festering places in our minds are like ulcers that affect our emotional life, our relationships with people, and eventually our business.

Wish Good Things For People

William Law said, "Love and pity and wish well to every soul in the world." You may not want to do this. You might be saying, "I'm not wishing jerks and criminals and sleezeballs well. Maybe I can wish good things for my skinny granny and my sweet girlfriend, but not the turnip nose who flaps his finger at me on the freeway."

Well, I'm going to tell you a secret. When you exempt certain people from your fine and loving thoughts and put negative thoughts on them instead, you will actually draw them, or people like them, *into* your life. It's almost like these people hustle in and say, "Here I am. I'm gonna' be a real stinker. See if you can love me."

Practice Loving People

And speaking of love, practice loving people. Sometimes, that's a hard one, but love will draw people to you, both strangers and people you already know. People are prospects, and prospects may turn into distributors.

Some of us have to start out by loving animals, then move into loving people. Once I had a boyfriend that adored his rabbit. He was sappy about that big white rabbit. He loved it more than any person. I understood, because I knew his background and how his mother had treated him. He was afraid to get close to a person and be hurt, but he figured a rabbit wouldn't bruise his heart. I hoped he'd eventually be able to transfer that unqualified love over to people. A sad thing happened, though. He went to such lengths to protect his love object that he killed it. Darrel was forever hauling that rabbit off to the vet. He got its ears cleaned, its fur scrubbed, and its pink nose droppered with ointments. That rabbit got shots to prevent every possible disease. I kept saying, "Darrel, leave that rabbit alone. You're gonna' kill it with all that doctoring." Darrel didn't think so.

However, the last time he took the rabbit to the vet was the last time he took the rabbit to the vet. The vet shot Mr. Rabbit full of some exquisite vaccinations that killed him. He tipped right over on the table and died. I thought Darrel would die, too. It was awful. Later, I got Darrel a brown and white puppy named Joker who quickly replaced me as the probable-number-one love object in his heart. Soon after, I moved on to a man who had graduated to loving people, but the story has a happy ending. Darrel must have been able to roll some of that rabbit and dog love over, because he found a nice girl and they got married. Sometimes I drive by their home now, and see his fluffy dog, Joker, sitting on the front porch wearing his sun glasses (glare hurts his eyes) watching the cars go by.

My own story about learning to love people is odd, too. I think I've always loved people, but about twelve years ago it started getting extreme. I was miserably married to a man who verbally and physically abused me. My personal life was dreary and gray, but I loved my work. I had a little herb shop where I kept myself busy counseling and assisting people with minor and terminal health problems. One day, a man and wife, two people I didn't know, walked through the door. I looked at them and knew they'd come for help. Suddenly, it felt like my chest blew open and my heart puffed up to the size of the room, reached out towards this couple, and dragged them to me. I was staggered over by love, compassion, and the desire to help. Needless to say, I gave these people every attention. As I always did, with everyone.

It wasn't for vast amounts of money that I did this

work. Often, my savings supported the business. I just liked to do it. I got enormous joy from being of service. Since then, I've thought that my herb business might have been what started opening up my heart.

In many other ways, I've continued to be of service to people, and my heart has continued to burst open rather regularly. Sometimes, it's so overwhelming and I'm so drenched with emotion that I think, "Is this God working through me, or are my hormones acting up?!"

Darrel's way of learning to love and relate to people was through animals. My way came from joyous service to others. (I emphasize *joyous* because I don't think grudging service will open anything.) Your way might be something different. Perhaps it's as simple as imagining how another person feels and thinks. Whatever it is, *you need to feel something for people in order to approach them as you would like to be approached, and for them to respond.* You need to *care* in order to be truly effective in multilevel, which is, after all, a people business.

Shantideva said, "The childish work for their own benefit, the Buddhas work for the benefit of others. Just look at the difference between them."

I like what he said. MLM, worked with good intentions, reflects the Buddha or Christ-like nature. It also builds a big, prosperous multilevel business!

Your Prospect List
Make a List

You've reviewed your attitude. Now you're ready to find the right people for your business. The first thing you need to do is make up a prospect list. This is a list of everyone you can think of who might possibly be interested in your products and/or your business. Put every likely person on this list, including people you would be nervous about contacting.

The idea is to find at least five strong people to place directly under you. You'll start hunting from this list. Other people will come into your life, later.

• Put Your Names in a Notebook

You might want to keep these names in a small notebook, something that you can carry with you. You'll find that names drop into your head at the oddest, most inconvenient times, and in the strangest places. If you think, "Oh, I'll write that name down later," you won't, because it will have flown out of your head again. I often get names and "brilliant" ideas in the shower! It makes me so mad. I've got scores of names rubbed into the walls with soap and I've had dozens of Pulitzer prize winning novels wash down the drain.

When I started my business, I used a yellow legal pad. I sat cross-legged on my bed, squeezed my eyes shut, and started remembering everyone I'd ever known. I remembered the old couple I'd visited and stayed with in Kansas when I was doing a talk for my previous multilevel years before. I remembered how those two had fought all weekend and worn me out. They'd fought about the business we were in. They'd been in it for years but weren't making enough money. I figured they were candidates for my new business.

I remembered a lady I'd known who had six kids and a small business in her home. Every time I called to order some of her stuff, a little kid grabbed the phone, breathed moistly into it, and hung up. I wasn't sure if my new business would thrive with her, but she was open to making money.

•Pull Out Your Little Black Book

I pulled out my old tattered address book from my first marriage. I'd lived on an air base and had a ton of friends. I'd been pregnant with my daughter and had taken time off from teaching school, so I just had fun.

Marcia

Marcia was my next door neighbor. Every morning I slid down the bank between our base houses and had coffee with her. One day she set out a huge canister of potato chips and I ate every one. Another time I ate an entire 9"x12" banana cake that she baked especially to go with our tea. I still felt embarrassed about my pregnancy eating excesses, and didn't think I'd call her.

Carolyn

Another friend from the base, Carolyn, was very interesting and enterprising. She lived in squalor. Her house was filled with every newspaper she'd received for two years. They were stacked in piles beside every chair, *on* most chairs, and tucked into couches. She said she might read them one day. Several parrots screamed from cages that hung from the ceiling, while bird feathers hung from everything. Piles of unemptied trash baskets lined the rooms, as did washed and unwashed clothes, flung together in piles of colors. All the knickknacks she'd collected in her air force travels were stacked on window ledges, bookcases, and counters. We girls viewed her home with awe and disgust and sat where we could.

When Carolyn wasn't collecting and stacking, she was busy pickling cucumbers and peppers, and canning beans and peaches, and any darn vegetable that struck her fancy. It was a charming habit and we, her friends, received most of her output. The problem was, we were afraid to eat the bounty. We saw how she kept her house, and felt that fastidiousness wouldn't show up in her canning practices either. We didn't want to end up dead. I don't know what the other girls did with their canned produce, but I couldn't imagine tossing food away. My concern about waste kept dozens and dozens of Carolyn's canned goods lined up on most of my closet and kitchen shelves throughout the house until we moved. Carolyn, I thought, might be a good choice for multilevel because she was so enterprising. I wrote her name down.

Maxine

Then there was Maxine. You could dab vanilla ice cream on her floors and lick it off without gagging. It would have been the same as eating off clean plates. I remember her telling me once about her marriage. Every evening her skinny-haired husband would come home and reach up and run his finger across the tops of the door jambs and windows to see if there was any dust. In my mind, that summed up the entire sorry relationship. If she was still with him, I was sure he wouldn't let her do multilevel. Too messy and unpredictable.

Marcie

Then I thought of Marcie, another friend on the base, a beautiful girl with glossy black hair. She'd had a baby boy and her husband bored her stiff. Marcie was petite and sweet, and Harry was fat and his lips hung over his chin. He said "Ump" a lot, and took long naps. Maybe she would be ready for a change by now.

I spent a good day or two remembering and writing down names on my legal pad. Every moment, I was thinking about people from my past and present.

Susan

I went back to college days and thought of my dorm

roommate, Susan. As much as I tried, I couldn't remember what she'd been studying or what she wanted to do with her future. All I could remember was her love life, which was a lot more interesting than mine. She had a steady boyfriend named Frank whom she later married, and they moved to Georgia. But while she roomed with me, she took birth control pills that made her grumpy and gave her insomnia. Every time I'd turn over in bed at night she'd yell, "Stop that! I can't sleep!" Which meant I couldn't sleep very well, either.

The funniest thing I remembered was when she and Frank were chased by space aliens. One night, just before midnight, Susan came flying and shrieking into our dorm room, her clothes half on and backwards, and her bleached blonde hair shooting out at stiff angles. "Wake up!" she yelled. "Frank and I were chased by flying saucers!"

I was awake and ready.

"We were under a bridge in our car," she gasped. "Oooh," she moaned, squeezing her eyes like she did when she was hormonally unbalanced, "we were. . .we were, well, petting, you know?" I looked blankly at her. "We were naked!" she snapped. "We were doing *it*, for God's sake!"

"Oooh." I said, knowing I should say something.

Susan broke down and started whimpering, "Right in the middle of *it*," she said, "a flying saucer came after us! We didn't see it, but it was the most eerie, most scary, outer space sound I've ever heard. Just like flying saucers sound in the space movies! Frank threw the car into gear and we took off, both of us totally naked. He drove a hundred miles an hour back to the dorm."

I could picture them both as naked as dogs without coats screaming down the roadways, past the college hot dog stand, past the school President's house, squealing to a halt at stop lights, then racing up to the well-lit dorm entrance.

"Did anyone see you naked?" I asked.

Susan looked at me like my head had shrunk.

"I don't know," she said coldly. "We're lucky to be alive."

Several weeks later I heard that space ship wail myself, although I had my clothes on at the time. It was a police car with a new type of siren. I guess if I'd been under a bridge when it went over, with all my clothes off, embroiled in an act of illicit passion, I too would have thought it was a space ship sent by the college officials to whisk me away for bad behavior. I thought I'd call Susan just for kicks.

You can have fun remembering and putting names on your list. In fact, it's a good idea to remember details, because you'll have a better idea of how to approach these people. The next step is harder. You have to contact these people.

Contact the People On Your List
•Immediately Identify Yourself

When I eventually got up my nerve and began calling people off my list, I identified myself immediately and said, "Hi, this is Venus. I know. You haven't heard from me in awhile (years!), but here's why I'm calling."

•Tell People Why You're Calling

I learned not to pretend that I was calling strictly for social reasons and then, at the end, suddenly admit that I wanted the person to do something for me, like drink ant juice or join my multilevel. People don't like to be flattered with our attention, then used.

• Ask if the Person is Busy

Ask if your friend is busy. If she is and you don't bother to ask, she'll resent your intrusion. It's sort of like what happened to me the other day. I was in a bookstore, paying for a book. The cashier was in the process of taking my money, getting my receipt, etc. I was in a hurry. Another lady popped up to the counter and said, "Oh, do you have any books by such and such an author?" The salesgirl immediately stopped helping me and flipped on her computer to search books for this woman. I watched, fascinated and annoyed, as she spent my time chatting with this lady. Finally, she announced, "Well, we've got two books here." The new customer said, "Okay. Never mind. I was just curious." And she walked off.

I felt the same way I would feel if someone called to tell me about this great multilevel and never bothered to ask if I was busy or rushed or if I even wanted to hear about it. I would feel intruded upon, and I'd feel that the caller was rude. A telephone caller should have the same manners as a person in the flesh.

• Write to Everyone on Your List

If you choose to write to the people on your list, you might send something simple, like a company brochure and a note. "Hi. Remember me? We went to school together in Mrs. Tuxwatum's math class. By the way, I finally did graduate! Hope you'll glance at this. It's what I'm doing now. I'll call in a day or two. We can chat about it and our love lives."

Or, maybe you'll send a letter: "Hi, I really want to talk to you about something I'm doing. You might be interested. I'll call in a day or two and we'll talk about it. And what ever happened to your old mother-in-law after she lost her false teeth down the park toilet?" It could be a longer letter introducing what you're doing with more background.

Many people want to send form letters. I don't do that. To me, that's not friendly and personal. I pay attention to mail written especially for me. I rarely look at form letters. If you insist on sending a form letter in order to save time, please add a handwritten note, at least.

• Don't Overwhelm Yourself

Here's something a lot of people forget. I know about it because I've done it, too. When I first started my business, I mailed letters to about thirty people at once with a note that said, in part, "I'll call you in a few days." Well, just try calling thirty people in a few days. It can stretch to weeks or longer, and meanwhile the person who received your stuff has forgotten all about it and you. Send your materials out in small batches. When you're about caught up, send a few more.

•Keep a Detailed List of People You Contact

Every time you mail something, be sure to keep a list of what you've sent, when you sent it, and who you sent it to. Leave space after each entry for the results of your contact. I used to send things out and maybe make a note of it on a scrap of paper, somewhere, which I usually lost. Later I would think, "Did I contact George? What did I send him? When? Did he care?"

•Think Before You Make Demands

I get letters every week that contain an MLM company's entire prospectus. The person writing will say, "I really value your opinion. I'm trying to decide if I'm in a good multilevel. Will you please examine the marketing plan and read about the products and let me know what you think?"

This may work with people who have puffy egos and little MLM experience, but it doesn't work with me anymore. I look at pages and pages of circles swinging off sticks with piles of numbers, and I blanch. I know the writer thinks I'll read all about his fabulous deal, realize I'll become a millionaire with this incredible marketing plan, and will call him excitedly to sign up in a frantic rush. Not so. I feel annoyed. I don't have the time to play these games. With me, it's far better to call first, or send a note asking if I'd like to see some information about such and such. I like honesty, and I think most other people do too.

Here's something I wouldn't do to a prospect: The other day, in the mail, I got a video. I was curious and I opened it up. A woman had enclosed a note, "Please watch this about my great multilevel company. I'll call in a few days to discuss it."

Listen, I try to be saintly and a helpful friend to all. I do my best to answer everyone who writes and calls me, and I genuinely like to do that and to help people. But that video annoyed me. Again, I don't have time to watch all these videos and listen to all these tapes that people send me because they want to get me in their downline. And then be expected to do it and be ready to discuss it when the person calls? I think I'm like everybody else. If I get mad about this, I know my prospects will, too. If I were you, and I had a hot video or a great audio, I'd *call* the prospect first and say, "May I send you this or that? Would you feel okay about watching (or listening to) it?"

First of all, the prospect has a choice. They have some

control over their lives and won't feel like a bad person if they don't do what you ask. Some people will even be honest with you and say, "Gee. I really wouldn't watch it." You'll save the price of your time, the video, and the postage. If someone says, "Well, I guess so," or, "Yeah, send it," then send it. They know it's coming and won't be upset when seeing it. They may even be curious.

Remember something: You're going to be contacting a lot of people off your prospect list, and you'll be lucky if you get one or a few people interested. It's a numbers game in multilevel. You'll hate it, but it's true. Just remember that all it takes is one hot distributor to make you wealthy.

Results From My Prospect List

Here's what happened with my list: I called the old couple that had argued the entire weekend I spent with them. They were the ones who hadn't made any decent money off their multilevel in all the years they'd been working it. I was sure they'd praise and bless me when I called to tell them I'd found something that would really work and make them a living. I called them, and after I'd outlined my discovery and what I felt their next move should be, there was a silence the size of Kansas. Then, they started yelling at me. The conclusion I came to after the haranguing was over was that they didn't appreciate being told that they'd wasted all those years in the wrong multilevel, and by dang, they were part of the best damn multilevel in the country, and just because they were out to help people and not rake in an ill-gotten fortune was no reason to think they were stupid and didn't know what they were doing. Or something along those lines. I was chastened and spent awhile thinking about my approach. I thought I'd better make some changes.

Next, I tried to call my old dorm mate, Susan, and the girls I'd met on the air base. Everybody had moved. Probably years before. They were all gone. Maybe married and divorced dozens of times with all kinds of name changes and I'd never find them again. I sat down and cried. I really missed those girls. Why hadn't I kept up with them? Because I'd been too involved in getting married and divorced myself, and making a living. I felt wretched. Too late, I'd learned another lesson. Friends are too important to let life and money get in the way.

There were others on my list and I called and wrote them with various results. I got mainly "No's" or polite evasions. Some people said, "Oh, okay," they'd try my stuff. Most never did. Eventually, I got a few retail people off the list and a few distributors. But after six months of pounding one lady, she joined me, and eventually built quite a business. The rest of my group came from other sources, which I'll go into later.

Keep a Prospect Notebook

This is different than the little notebook you're carrying around to record names in. My prospect notebook is a small spiral-bound school notebook. When I get to the point with a prospect where I've sent her product, or given or sent her brochures, videos, and/or audios, and she's given me some response and we're continuing to keep in touch, I give her a page to herself in this notebook. I write down the date our contact started, her name, phone number, address, what I've given her, what she's said, and what I've said. Each time there's a contact, I write it down with the date, so I'll remember. Many, many people stay in this book and never go further. When someone, however, becomes a distributor, I put a big "D" on the page and rip it out of the notebook. (That's a good feeling!) Then I transfer that page to my *New Distributor Folder*.

•Keep a New Distributor Folder

My folder is green, to symbolize money. I tape the smaller sheet with the person's name and all the data I've collected on him onto an 8 1/2"x11" sheet of paper. I continue to write down all contact and what is given, said, or done. I keep these people in a New Distributor Folder so I remember to work with them constantly for awhile. How long? Until they show me they're not going to do anything, or much, or until they graduate to a higher level.

REVIEW
Your Prospect List

1. Make a List
  - *Put Your Names in a Notebook*
  - *Pull Out Your Little Black Book*

2. Contact the People On Your List
  - *Immediately Identify Yourself*
  - *Tell People Why You're Calling*
  - *Ask if the Person is Busy*
  - *Write to Everyone on Your List*
  - *Don't Overwhelm Yourself*
  - *Keep a Detailed List of People You Contact*
  - *Think Before You Make Demands*

3. Keep a Prospect Notebook
  - *Keep a New Distributor Folder*

CHAPTER 2

THE IDEAL PROSPECT

Look for Real People, Not Slick MLM Wheeler-Dealers

Let me tell you how I spent this past weekend. I drove to a big city for a multilevel seminar sponsored by a multilevel magazine. I was there to autograph books and smile and beam at the public. The day was supposedly every distributor's dream. I, however, met more slick fellows than you could cram into a hot air balloon. Oddly enough, it's generally men who fall into this category. I've known a few women of this type, but the men far outnumber the ladies. I spent my day listening to every pitch and wild, ego-stuffed story you could think of. I met a number of fellows who said, "Hi, I'm the president of a multilevel company."

"Oh," I'd say, "which one?"

"Well," the man would admit as he leaned back in his chair and sucked on a cigarette, "I haven't named it, yet." And, as it would turn out, he hadn't decided on the products to distribute, he didn't have the start-up money either, and no, he didn't know when the whole thing would come together.

I had multitudes of men loping and hovering beside and around me all day. And they weren't struck by my beauty—they were presenting their businesses to me, hoping to snatch me into their downlines. Some were brazen about it, "I'm a top distributor for the one multilevel that's going to sweep the world, and you'll never be sorry if you sign with me!" and some were sneaky. One round-bodied, round-headed older man presented himself as a consultant to all the major companies. He'd just, he assured me, laid out the entire plan for a new multilevel company, and they were following his every suggestion. "That's amazing," I said. "I'm amazed that they'd do everything you tell them to do."

"Oh, yes," he said, "everything. And because they're doing what I tell them to do, they're going to be the biggest thing that ever hit. Sit down here." He swept a table clear in a grand gesture, whipped out a chair, pushed me into it, then sat himself down across the table from me. "Let me show you something," he said, "about this company." He proceeded to boldly write out the marketing and compensation plan, how much I'd make, and how I could sign right now. I figured out pretty quickly that he was a distributor for this company, or even the president (which would explain why the company did everything he said), and was trying to recruit me. I was disgusted. Another fellow, Hank, kept plying me with flyers on his company and products. Every half hour he had a new batch, and when I finally escaped the melee, I found another wad of Hank's brochures under my car's window wipers.

These kinds of people will try to convince you that the only way to be what's called a "Big Hitter" in multilevel is to sign up people like themselves. I disagree. These types are often full of loose wires and wind and they all spin in circles together, each trying to outtalk, outhype, and outshine each other. They generally talk in numbers and not words, and tend to overwhelm lesser folk like you and me.

•Real People

I've had better luck with old ex-hippies, grandmothers, followers of various saints, housewives, mothers, and cowboys. Real people. Offbeat people. People who think for themselves, and people who approach others in a real, human way. People who know how to form and cultivate long-running relationships. People who see beyond the money and tinsel and stacks of numbers, and who truly want to help others succeed. I look for people who are willing to spend the time it takes, the energy it takes, and the persistence it takes to build a solid, long-running business. I suspect that the wheeler-dealers I met at the seminar I just discussed are sincere in their own way. They want to succeed, but I bet most of their energy is spent thinking about the numbers and the money and the big cars and little airplanes they're going to get and "stacking this person on top of that one, and then putting Charlie here and he'll get 16 cases and that'll get me a trip to Havana if Pearl gets her sister to sign in," etc. This kind of thinking and dealing works for some people. But not for most of us. I think it scares and unnerves us. From what I've seen, most of us don't even have minds like that. And if you don't think like that, how many people do you think you can put in your downline who will be like that?

Friends, Family, and Strangers

Let's discuss other types of people you might be looking at for your business. Most people start with their friends and family, who are usually regular people, types who might prosper in multilevel. Unfortunately, your friends and family know you so well that they often think you don't know anything. I like strangers much better, because they often think I know more than they do. They'll think the same about you.

•Relatives Can Be a Real Challenge

Some people do well at recruiting family, so don't cross family off because of my experiences. I just find that lots of people have the same troubles with their relatives that I've had with mine. For example, a few years ago, I'd just gotten back from a company training in Palm Springs. I was all hyped up and excited, ready to recruit anyone who could breathe and whistle. I figured that this was the time to lay it on my sister, Polly, again. I'd always tried through the years to recruit her, but although she has supported me in every other way, she was thoroughly resistant, even violent, about not joining me in multilevel.

Today, I felt, was The Day. Her last chance. She and my brother Jim were meeting me in the patio of a local restaurant. Surely, I felt, I could snag Jim, too.

Well, perhaps that day wasn't the best day after all. I *was* tired, exhausted really, from the trip and all the hoopla. I wasn't at my best. I was a little short tempered. In fact, a bit touchy. A bit fed up with Polly's stalling and snide remarks about my business and products over the years. In fact, I felt down right angry about her lack of positive response, and by golly, today she was going to see it my way.

She didn't. In fact, I'm embarrassed to tell you that we had a huge fight, right on the restaurant patio, among the ice teas, the flies, and the local townfolk, most of whom knew us.

I'd worked on Polly for a good five years. A few months before, I'd even gotten her to try one of my Wonderful Products, but she protested that it tasted like dragon piss and that her chiropractor had said he saw no earthly use for the Wonderful Product. Now, she was yelling at me, "Don't even talk to me about that stuff! Get it off the table! Get it away from me! I don't want to look at it!"

I couldn't help myself. Like a maniac who goes berserk while everyone says, "Oh, I can't believe it. He seemed like such a nice, quiet, unassuming man, the last person in the world to shoot his wife and kids and then level the post office!" I went berserk. I became that maniac, screaming that my little gray-haired, sweet-smiling sister Polly was a pink-shirted, snotty-stuffed, toad-headed person and I was tired of her stupid remarks and superiority and condescending attitude and I'd had enough of it. I yelled that I was still mad about the time when we were little and our parents left me to baby sit all the kids and she immediately ran me up a tree with a broom and kept me there all day, and that I was fed up with her controlling, bossy ways!

"Oh my," my pretty little sister mumbled. "Oh my."

Jim was shrinking back in his chair and whispering, "Oh, wow. Oh wow."

The locals didn't say anything.

I finished what had started out as my product and marketing demonstration to Polly by saying, "Well. I guess you're not right for this business," and then we all had lunch.

I've been in multilevel for fourteen years on and off, and out of two parents and five brothers and sisters, I've never managed to sign anyone. Ditto for all the cousins and other odd relations. And I'm considered to be a whopping success in multilevel. If your record approaches mine, don't feel bad.

I've managed to sign friends, but I've found that the closer the friend, the more resistant they are to my entreaties.

But, strangers? Let me at 'em.

Reconsider Your Least Likely Prospects

Remember that *everyone* is a possible prospect. It's just hard to know who'll really do anything. What makes the evaluating most difficult is that the person who seems most unqualified is, occasionally, the one who ends up building a great business. Here's a lurid example of that:

I met Jack a year and a half before I signed him. I met him in rather inauspicious circumstances. I still refer to our first meeting as my *New Year's Eve In Hell*. My younger brother Jim insisted that I come with him to the "greatest New Year's Eve party" I'd ever attend. He and a bunch of friends had rented a big van and were ferrying themselves out of our tiny mountain town and down to the big city of San Diego. "It'll be a blast," Jim promised. "We're going to a jumping place to eat a huge meal and party right in the heart of the city."

I know Jim, and I know what his idea of a "great party" can be. I was suspicious. My brother had owned his own restaurant and was past president of the Chamber of Commerce in town. He is well known, and everybody loves him. Jim also loves everybody, but sometimes this means he has little to no discrimination when it comes to friends and parties. I said I'd pass on his party invitation.

Well, Jim begged and pleaded. For some reason he wanted me to be there. Since my only other options were a singles sit-down dinner with strangers, or staying at home with my animals, I finally said yes. It was nice to feel wanted.

New Year's Eve came and so did Jim and the group. I was there to meet them at the gate. I heard the van and the "gang" rolling up my long dirt driveway before I saw them. It sounded like a loose bunch of banshees. As the new van rolled to where I stood, I noticed it had all its windows painted with obscene sayings about the riders. My name was featured prominently. The door slid open and I tried to enter, but was prevented by four drunk men who tumbled out onto my driveway, picked themselves up, then raced to pee copiously and with great spirit on my wooden fence.

"Hey!" Jim yelled to me. "Come on in."

This was the start of my night in hell. The drive through the mountains with the local ruffians (the President of the board of Realtors, two ex-Chamber Presidents, and assorted business owners) convinced me that I didn't want to go through with the evening. The only one sober, besides me, was the driver, thank God, and another fellow named Jack. When we made a stop half an hour later, I dragged Jim behind the van and said, "I'm going home. Find me a way. I don't care what it costs!"

Jim was apologetic and embarrassed. "Please," he said, "you're gonna' love it. Just humor me. You need to get out." Since there wasn't a realistic way home, I stomped around, flapped my arms a bit, and acquiesced.

At our next stop (somebody needed to throw up), we

all piled out of the van again. As I stood shaking and silent in the cold night air, Jack sidled up to me. He was in his twenties, good-looking, and sober. "Ah, ahem. . ." he started, "I don't really know these guys." He looked at the ground. "I'm from Iowa. I just got here."

"My brother is one of them," I said. "I should have known better."

The rest of the long night was more of the same, but eventually, I just gave up and joined in. At the restaurant, on one drink, I managed to dance on the tables, swish my way through all the shattered beer bottles on the floor, fight for my turn at the toilets, and generally confound all Jim's friends with my amazing switch in personality.

I also got Jack interested in my business.

For a full year and three months, I kept after him with product samples and literature. I didn't press him too hard, because I didn't think he had what it takes to build a business, but he kept bringing it up. I had doubts because he was quite young, single, didn't seem to have any ambition except working out at the gym, and he had been in that van that night, even if he was from Iowa.

Every time I'd think, "Well, that's it. I'm not fooling with him anymore," he'd spot me in town, run over, and say he was still interested in the business. Finally, for whatever reasons, he signed with me.

At that point, when we sat and talked for about half an hour, I was stunned. This guy was excellent multilevel material. He'd been skinny in college, he said, and he was determined to change that. He'd joined a gym and made it his life until he reached his goal. He'd had lots of experience making cold calls, and had successful businesses behind him. He said, "I'm telling you all this so you'll know I'm serious and that I've decided to really build something here."

I said, "I'm glad, Jack. But, honestly, I never saw those abilities in you, probably because of our rotten beginning."

Jack looked shy and embarrassed. "I guess I can tell you this, now," he said. "Jim told me all about you before that New Year's night. He told me how successful you were and how you'd written books and were famous. I really, really wanted to make a good impression on you. I decided before I ever met you that I wanted to sign up with you. And then," he glanced at me, "we drove to your place, and the first thing those guys did was jump out and pee on your fence! I couldn't believe it! I thought, 'Oh no! She'll always think I'm a jerk, now!' That's why I've waffled so much with you. I've been embarrassed, but hoping that eventually you'd think better of me!"

That's my story with Jack. It proves that you never know who'll be good and who won't be, for various, and even strange, reasons.

Be Selective

You may think you want to sign up your entire church congregation or everyone who drives the freeways or shops at your grocery store, but do you really think this is a good idea? What do you know about these people? Do you want to take the chance of being stuck with them the rest of your life? Think about some people you work with now. What if they were on the phone to you every day complaining about their business and whining about how their kids treat them and telling you that you're a lousy upline and demanding that you find them some decent distributors?

Sara

One of my downline, Nancy, signed a woman named

Sara. Sara found fault with the company, the products, with me, and with Nancy. Sara constantly called and harassed Nancy with foolish questions and complaints. I kept telling Nancy to get rid of her, that she wasn't worth her shattered peace of mind. Nancy would cry and say, "But, I can't. She's my downline."

I used to sign up everybody who asked or that I could talk into the deal. I did that, I think, because it took me three months to figure out how to sign anybody up, and I was so grateful and glad that I went on a recruiting binge. I was sorry later, because I had loads of people who never did anything but worry me and take up my time.

Gradually, I became selective. The first lady I turned down, Ethel, got my number from my sister. Yep. From Polly. She was probably getting even with me for the restaurant scene.

Ethel

Ethel came out to see me. She was an old seventy-five and wanted to stay all day. She just wanted a nice chat and a visit and she wanted to become a distributor to assure herself that she could visit and chat everyday. I don't have time for that. Plus, she wasn't quite quick-witted anymore. For several hours, she told me how she'd planted her iris bulbs upside down last spring. Then I heard about the crazy birds in her cherry trees and the good old days when she'd had a great figure and all the men liked her. Then, amidst all the babble, she'd assure me that once she'd signed up with me, she'd buy twelve cases of product, and she had a ton of friends that would sign, too. It was tempting, but I resisted. I sent her to my upline, whom she signed up with, and wouldn't you know, she bought twelve cases! However, with those twelve cases, my upline, Diane, had to visit with Ethel every day and constantly hear about those up-side-down bulbs and the boys who liked her figure.

Money isn't everything. Time is more valuable.

I repeat: It's difficult to know who will and who won't make a success of the business. Even old pros have trouble with that one. However, some people are such blatant "No's" that you need to learn to resist them.

REVIEW
The Ideal Prospect

1. **Look for Real People, Not Slick MLM Wheeler-Dealers**
   - *Real People*
2. **Friends, Family, and Strangers**
   - *Relatives Can Be a Real Challenge*
3. **Reconsider Your Least Likely Prospects**
4. **Be Selective**

CHAPTER 3

FINDING PROSPECTS:
WHAT TO DO, WHERE TO GO

Now that you've run through your prospect list, you're probably wondering what else you can do and where you can go to find likely prospects. Here are a few ideas that have worked for me.

1. Restaurants

This morning, on my way home from an early breakfast meeting, I stopped to see my folks. They live by the side of the road in a one hundred-year-old white farmhouse, surrounded by frowzy eucalyptus trees and screaming peacocks. My brother Jim was there, upstairs with our parents, having breakfast and recounting his latest adventures. I settled down at the old round table as the four of us pensively stared out the window. The day was gray and dripping. We collectively sighed and wished for the sun.

"How's the restaurant business?" I said to Jim.

"Well," he replied, "I probably won't be there much longer. I'm ready to open my travel business as soon as I get the building refurbished. Although," he continued. "I think I'm gonna' miss being a temporary waiter."

I patted his stylish haircut and remarked on his neatly trimmed beard. He's a handsome guy. "So, what will you miss?" I asked. "You said the restaurant is full of multilevelers and they're driving you crazy."

"Oh!" he laughed and snorted. "That's what I'll miss! Venus, you just have to come down there and see them in action. I never saw anything like it!"

"I don't think so," I said.

"Come on," Jim begged. "You could write about it. I'm telling you, this restaurant is their *hangout*. They're all with the same company, and I'd swear you'd think they were all a bunch of evangelists. It's so funny. They all wear dark suits, wild ties, and big hair. They must drink five or six cups of coffee a night, and this is at eleven at night! They're wired up all the time. And they all call me 'Jimmy.' They say, 'How ya' doing tonight Jimmy?' And they pop up from the table and pump my hand. 'You're looking good tonight, Jimmy. Sit down for a minute, Jimmy. I have an interesting offer for you.'

"I look at 'em and say, 'Geez, you say this to me every night. You guys know you'll never get me in multilevel. My sister has tried for years and even she can't get me.'"

"That's for sure," I say.

"And the women are the same way, Venus. They always hop up and say, 'Good evening Jimmy,' then they look me straight in the eye and give my hand a good, firm shake."

I'm laughing at the picture of all these serious multilevelers, persistent for months now, all in pursuit of and driven to sign up my reluctant brother.

"They're always so *up*," Jim says. "Always pumped.

Everything is wonderful. The money is great, the plan is great, the company is great. They say things like, 'Gee! Wasn't that a glorious seminar we had last weekend! Glorious!' They actually use words like 'glorious,' 'stupendous,' and 'sensational.' If anybody dares to probe someone else about their monthly check or question the marketing plan, somebody quick! grabs 'em and hauls 'em off to a table with just the two of them, where out comes all the graphs and charts and circles and numbers. And, what's really funny," Jim slaps the table and hoots, "is I see them all drive up to the restaurant in these old beaters! Then, they trot inside and haul out their airplane and fast car magazines and start going through them. As each guy comes in, they take note and say things like, 'Ah, I see, Howard, you're looking at Lamborginis, or Cessnas,' or whatever. And, they're serious!" Jim's voice goes up several incredible octaves.

"I guess," I say, "they're playing the Fake It 'Till You Make It game."

I'm thinking that it's good to think positively and envision what you want, but I have a feeling that's not what's happening here.

"Yeah," Jim says. "And you should see them prospecting. Everyone who comes into the restaurant is a prospect. They go table to table, being friendly, shaking hands, chatting, and usually they even manage to slide the customers in the booth over and slip in with them! This goes on all night long. And they never give up on me. Their favorite line is to cock their head at me, get a perplexed yet caring look on their faces and say, 'So Jimmy. What exactly is it that's kept you out of multilevel?' Well, truthfully," Jim laughs, "it's watching them every night!"

"Do they ever sign anybody up?" I ask.

"Oh, sure," Jim says. "Lots of people. All the Navy guys come to this restaurant. They're bored, lonesome, would like to make some money and have a part in the community, so yeah, they get a lot of people. Then, pretty soon those people are wearing dark suits, wild ties, and big hair!"

"I guess their technique is working," I say. "But, if nobody is making any money, then the whole thing seems kind of pointless."

"Well, they sure have a good time," Jim says. "And I hate to admit it, but I'll miss 'em. I think they'd do all right if they just got in another multilevel and were a little more themselves. That's the trouble. They all act like each other and like their company expects them to, and they pretend everything's hunky-dory all the time. They're really funny. They're a bunch of coffeed-up clones."

"But," I said, "maybe one way to meet people is to go to a particular restaurant that has lots of prospects and just keep going until you fit in there. And be friendly."

Jim just looks at me. He's anxious to start his travel business and hopes I'm not still expecting him to do multilevel! He'll always be leery of me.

There are lots of ways to find distributors. Besides hanging out in restaurants, here are some more ideas:

2. The Beach, the Mall, the Circus, the Grocery Store, Etc.

Sharon lives right near the beach. The other day she said, "I've taken my weight loss stuff to all the chiropractors and trade shows and marathons and conventions I can locate. It hasn't worked. There's too much competition. But, I'm looking out my window here at the beach and there are fat people lying all over it! How can I get to them? I know they're embarrassed about their blubber and cellulite hanging out of all those tiny tight suits."

I thought a moment and said, "Why don't you write up a survey? Say you're testing some new products and you would like to ask a few questions about the person's eating habits, or whatever. Carry your beach tote with you, full of product. Whip out a weight loss bar and say, 'Would you eat something like this?' Read the label to them, then compare it to others. Tell what it's done for you. Look earnest and say, 'Would you like a bite?'

"When they say, 'Where can I get some?' you say, 'Oh, I can get it for you. In fact, I've got some boxes in the car I was taking to my Old Aunt Toot. She can wait.'

"By trying this," I told Sharon, "you may pick up some retail customers and a few distributors."

You don't have to live near a beach to do this. Fat people are everywhere. However, I don't think it's wise to approach fat people with a fat survey. Maybe you can call it an energy foods survey, or whatever it is that your company specializes in.

3. Garage Sales

Larry and John do something a bit different that they assure me works stupendously well. I call them The Galloping Garage Sale Guys. On Saturday and Sunday mornings, they get up with the sun. They stick on their company buttons, which say something about dieting, or money, or herbs, or water filters, whatever, and head out for two days of sauntering through garage sales. Larry says, "Not just any garage sale, Venus. We go to the exclusive neighborhoods where the owner has enough money to buy our products or might have an interest in a new business. John and I just hang around awhile. I'll pick up an ashtray or unique pen set and say, 'John, how do you ya' think this would look in our home office?'

"Or, I'll hold a lamp in the air, squint a bit and say, 'Hey, John, how about this in the corner where you write up all your bank deposits?' Pretty soon the owner is asking us what we do for a living and we go on from there. It's a great way to spend a weekend, and we get prospects."

4. Barn Sales

Mary, on the other hand, holds what she calls "barn sales." She has a red barn stuffed with her multilevel products and assorted household rejects. She lives up a dirt road, next to a big church. Periodically, she asks the church members to contribute to these sales, they advertise together, then sit and wait. Mary says she moves a lot of product this way and signs people up. The church makes money off their stuff and everybody's happy. The only problem, Mary says, is that sometimes it rains and prospects can't get up her dirt road. But, on the positive side, sometimes they try, and get stuck, and when Mary and her husband go out to help them, they have a captive audience for awhile.

5. Bake, Estate, and Antique Sales

You may not have a barn, but you could have a garage or bake sale. You could also frequent estate sales or antique book sales. The key here is to figure out how to meet people. That's what we're doing with all these suggestions, just finding ways to meet and talk to people.

6. Classes and Seminars

Classes and seminars are excellent places to meet

people. Hubert tells me he's busy right now going to video classes every Thursday night. He has the excitement of hanging out in a TV studio for four classes while he builds trust with the other students. It's easy, from there, to mention what he does for a living and see if there's an interest.

7. Community Work

Candy is actively involved in community work after her long days as a teacher. "Teaching is killing me," she says. "I never have time for myself, and I like to work for the community. I meet all the people who get out and do things. These are just the people I need for the multilevel I'm building. The multilevel that's going to get me out of teaching."

Right now, Candy's involved in setting up a townwide neighborhood watch system. The committee she's on has divided up the town into sections, and then she and others act as block captains who go door-to-door meeting and re-meeting all the neighbors in each area. Re-meeting is the key. As Candy gets to know everyone, and sees them over time, it will be easy to mention what her sideline is. She's protecting her neighborhood and also prospecting.

8. Clubs and Organizations

If you're brave enough for this one, you can always speak to clubs and organizations. They're always looking for speakers, and if you'll speak for free, they'll let you talk, pretty much, about what you want to talk about. Don't make your advertisements too blatant, but in order to speak for nothing, you have to get something out of it. For example, let's say your company's products are environmentally friendly. Talk about the dangers of all the products that aren't and what they're doing to our environment. Maybe you just happen to have little brochures about your healthy products and company tucked beside everybody's plates. If you're touting security devices, talk security. Do demonstrations. If you sell herbal products, talk herbs. Be creative. Dream up something fun and interesting. To make it more appealing, you usually get a free lunch or breakfast at these meetings.

To find clubs and organizations, check your local paper or go see the Chamber of Commerce. The Chamber has lists of organizations. Call these groups. Say, "Do you ever need free speakers? I can speak about ———— , and I'd love to do it."

Trust me. They'll love hearing from you.

9. Wrong Numbers and Telephone Solicitors

I remember a fellow named Roger who picked up a solid distributor from a wrong number. The fellow thought he was calling his girlfriend and got Roger. Roger held on to him like a pitbull. "He'd disturbed me at dinnertime," Roger said, "and I decided to make it worth the interruption. I said, 'You sound like someone I know. What's your name? No, that doesn't ring a bell, but you sure sound familiar. Where do you work? Oh. Never heard of that place. Do you like it there? No? Ummm. Maybe you've met me? I sell security devices. They're real hot right now, you know. I kinda' fell into it. Gawd, I'm making fabulous money. Have you ever heard of ————?'"

Roger talked awhile longer, set up an appointment to meet the fellow, and eventually signed him.

You can do the same with telephone solicitors. Most telephone solicitors don't like their jobs, but they're sure getting good experience while doing it. They'd be perfect for your business. Ask if they'd like to hear about something that has the potential for making a lot more money than telephone soliciting and is easier and more fun. They should listen. After all, they've interrupted your life by barging electronically into your home without an invitation, and they owe you a courtesy.

10. "Solicitors Wanted"

I like to kid around and say, "Put a 'Solicitors Wanted' sign in your living room window, or on your front gate." But why not? The poor folks who trudge door-to-door will be surprised by it, but the truth is, you've got something great for these people. Let them in. Let them rub dirt into your rugs and suck it back out with a vacuum bottle of Wonder Spray. Regale them with the merits of your multilevel while they do so. Fair's fair.

11. Door-to-Door

Consider becoming a solicitor yourself with your products and business opportunity. Going door-to-door can bind your stomach in knots, of course, since facing strangers like this is intimidating, which is why most people don't do it. Since most people don't, won't, and can't do it, there is almost no competition. Maybe you ought to consider it? You'll meet lots of people.

Here are some ideas that may help you from my door-to-door experiences: When I was in real estate, I had a territory that I had to "farm." This meant that I was expected to drive out to this neighborhood and walk the streets every week. The idea was to get acquainted with the home owners, get them to like me, then beg them to list their homes with me when they were ready to move.

Farming that neighborhood was an ordeal. I had what were called the Flower Streets: Aster St., Blue Bonnet St.,

Carnation St., Daisy St., etc. If it sounds like an easy run through a field of flowers, it wasn't. It was a dingy area, loaded with renters, old rusted campers on the backs of dented black pickups, brown stucco houses, pale dry grass, and cracked baby toys strewn under skinny trees.

The householders liked to stay inside their houses, complain about the heat, drink beer from cans, and fight among themselves.

The first time I went calling, I parked my car and sat a moment to gather up my courage. I think I sat too long, because the sun slipped behind a little hill and I decided it was too late to bother people.

The second time, I went early, parked my car, and sat awhile again to find the courage that I seemed to have misplaced. This time, I decided, I'd come too early. People wouldn't be up yet, I reasoned, or they would be doing their household chores. It would be best to come back later.

Several times, the weather was too bad to walk, or the cheese sandwich I'd eaten had probably poisoned me and I couldn't image asking someone to let me in their home so I could throw up in their toilet.

After about a month of dry runs, I actually did get out of my car and walk the streets. To my great joy and vast relief, I discovered that almost no one was home. I'd ring a doorbell or tap tentatively on a screen door. Nothing. Thank goodness. I'd hop off the step and dance down the walk, feeling like I'd accomplished a great deal.

Eventually, I found that on weekends the houses held more people. However, the looks on people's faces when they opened the door and found me standing there with real estate flyers in my hands would have smashed a Viking's spirit.

After several weeks of torture on all our parts, I developed something that worked. As soon as someone opened the door and saw me, I grinned and said brightly, "I know you don't want to see me!" This threw the person off their frigid stance and as they straightened up in befuddlement, I'd lope into my little real estate spiel. The householders seemed both charmed and baffled, which I felt was better than their former annoyed and impatient attitudes. I'd broken through their congealed dislike of solicitors by saying outright what they were thinking.

Gradually, we began to develop relationships, which I hoped would lead to their automatically thinking of me when it came time to list their homes.

To hurry the process along and to reach the people I could never find at home, or who were hiding behind their couches when they saw me coming, I developed a marvelous plan. I would write a newsletter. Many real estate people did this, but mine would be different. Instead of interest rates and recipes for peach cobbler, I'd write about a consuming passion of mine—herbs and health. I'd make it interesting, too, something they'd have to read until the end, where they'd find my name, the name of the real estate company I worked for, my telephone number, and a frank plea for their listings and loyalty.

I wrote a meaty, descriptive, and detailed newsletter. It was clever and sharp and I knew it would be so entertaining that the Flower street householders would look forward to every edition. Carefully, I typed, photocopied, and folded up at least 250 and spent a morning depositing them in mailboxes. This would render my competition insensible. Why hadn't anyone done something so creative before this? I went back to my office and sat back to wait for calls and comments.

The first was from my boss, Al, the man who owned

and ran our office, an Italian with a flat head, a wife, two kids, and a girlfriend. I noticed him looking at me from his glassed-in cubicle at the south side of the office. He was on the phone. When he hung up, he kept looking at me. Then, still looking, he rose from his padded chair and waved me to him.

"Did you pass out a newsletter in the Flower streets?" he asked as I fluttered into his domain.

"Yes!" I said, delighted that he'd been informed about my hard work.

"That was the postal inspector," he said. "Putting flyers in mailboxes is a federal offense."

"Yea Gods!" I cried.

"You could go to jail," my boss said.

"Oh, no!" I said. "I'm too young." (Why I thought you had to be older to go to jail escapes me now that I'm older.)

I was terrified. Jail. Going to jail for putting flyers in mailboxes! I was an accidental criminal, and I'd pay for my stupidity.

"I told him you wouldn't do it again," my boss said dryly.

Thank God. Thank you God.

The next day, I looked up from the work on my desk. There stood my boss. "You know those flyers you put out, yesterday?" he said. A toothpick dangled from his lips.

"Yes?" I said.

"I've had a number of calls about them from people in the neighborhood."

I smiled broadly. I was a genius.

"They hate them," he said.

"They hate them?" I repeated. He must be mistaken, I thought.

"Did you write about parasites?" Al asked.

"Well, yes, " I admitted.

"Something about 95% of the population having worms and then describing what they look like? Something about black ones with red eyes and fangs? Something about how to get them out of your body with herbs?"

I was silent.

"Several of the women who called," Al said, "were hysterical." He chewed pensively on the toothpick. "All the callers never want to see that newsletter again."

Well, they never did, but I still considered myself a success. I'd gotten people to read the newsletter, and for darn sure, I thought, they'd remember me when it came time to list their houses!

You might consider taking your products and business opportunity door-to-door, but remember, go on the weekends when people are home, be natural when speaking to them, and throw them off guard a bit with your guilelessness. Consider a newsletter or product samples, but for heaven's sake, don't put them in mail boxes or talk about worms!

A distributor I know is a true genius at door-to-door work. When things are slow, he packs up some brochures and samples and heads out to a neighborhood. He taps on doors and when someone answers, he'll take a long hard look at them and say, "Say. . .would you be interested in some liquid energy?"

Before they have a chance to comment, he clicks his tongue and shakes his head. "No," he announces, I don't think you would."

Then, he turns to leave. Most of the time, the puzzled, rejected homeowner says, "Wait. Wait a minute. What do you mean?" That's Ed's cue to pull out his little bottle of energy brew, give it a shake in front of them, and launch into his talk and taste test. He sells and signs a lot of people this way.

If you decide to go door-to-door, remember, as with anything else in multilevel, door-to-door takes a lot of practice until you find what works for you.

• Cold Calls

The only time I've done cold calling is, again, when I was in real estate. That cured me. I can do cold calls, and I actually got quite good at it, but I've never been able to reconcile myself to barging in on strangers by telephone. In multilevel, the coldest call I do now is to call a prospect or customer for one of my downline. I tell my downline, "I'll call anybody to help you out, but I have one rule. You must tell the person who I am, that I'll be calling, and why." This way the distributor's prospect isn't caught unaware, and isn't quite as snotty to me.

12. Telephone Books and Purchased Mailing Lists

Some people build their businesses strictly from cold calls. They'll haul out a telephone book, or buy a list of names off a purchased mailing list and get to it. If you choose to do this, just remember that you generally need to contact a person five times in five different ways before you gain their trust. Instead of building a relationship in person, you have to do it by voice alone. You'll have to develop some kind of closeness. You'll need to think of reasons to re-call the possible prospects a second, third, and fourth time. You also have to show your personal interest in them. I mean real interest too, not fake.

13. Airplanes

Once I was on an airplane, seated next to a beautiful lady named Rebecca. I'm not a person who hustles everyone all the time. However, if I sense I have a prospect, I ask questions. I grin a lot while I do this, to keep their guard down. "Where are you going?" I asked. (Grin, grin.) "What kind of work do you do there? Do you like it? How's your love life?" (Yes, I really asked about her love life. Women hop into people's personal lives pretty darn fast. We can build a relationship with a person in five minutes if we have to. And personal relationships build this business.)

By the end of our five hour flight (and I only spoke to her for about a half hour, total — there was no sense wearing her, or myself, out), I had learned everything I needed to know. She was an actress looking for work, with a background in radio, health, and nutrition. She was getting a divorce, had a new boyfriend, and was moving out to my area. She also desperately needed a job to support her while she hunted for more TV work. I *didn't* say, "Oh! You must build a multilevel business! I have just the one for you!" That would have made her recoil from me. No one likes to feel forced into something, especially if they're trapped in the seat beside you. Instead, I said, "I totally understand about needing a job while you look for the work you really want to do. I had the same problem. I got lucky and built a big multilevel business that gives me the freedom to write books, like I always wanted to do." Then, I proceeded to suggest interim jobs that might pull her through, like waitressing, computer work, or maybe another radio show like she'd had before. We kicked around a bunch of ideas for her. Then I said, smiling blandly, "Yep, I'm really lucky. I found a good multilevel company with good products." I mentioned the company name and what the products were. She'd heard good things about it and them. Great. I let it rest. As our flight ended, I said, "Look, here's my card. Give me a call when you come to San Diego. We can have tea. And, give me your card, too. I like you and we can be friends. At least you'll know someone out here." Rebecca was thrilled and promised she'd call. And she did.

A month later we had lunch and talked about our love lives, our regular lives, and her job search. Toward the end of the meal, she asked how my business was doing. I told her, then casually said, "I always carry a few samples in my purse." (Actually, placed in there that very morning expressly for her!) "Here. Take them. See what you think." I then regaled her with a few exciting testimonials. Later, as we left the restaurant, I said, "Maybe you'll fall in love with this stuff and want to use it forever. Maybe you'll want to get it to some of your friends and make some money off it, like I do. After all, you're looking for an income. But, " I added, "it's okay if you don't want to do that. I'll never push you."

"Well, you know," Rebecca said, "I've always been interested in health."

You don't have to be on an airplane to meet a Rebecca. You could find her in a classroom, or any place where you have some time to chat.

Here's something I feel is important: I like the people I prospect. Even if Rebecca had never joined the multi-level, I would still want her in my life as a friend.

14. Elevators
Once, I'd forgotten myself and was wearing a multi-level company's button. Buttons that say something catchy

work well at grabbing a stranger's comments and attentions. I don't generally wear them, only because I like to choose whom I prospect. This particular day, however, I was in a hotel at a multilevel convention and was wearing the most recent button.

As I entered an elevator, an older lady and her granddaughter standing inside both pointed at my shirt and said in tandem, "What is that button? What does that mean? Why are all you people wearing those? What's going on?"

Well, you don't have much time in elevators, so I said, "Do you have any health problems?" (You could say, "Do you drink water, cook in aluminum, like pretty jewelry, need a cheaper phone system, would you feel safer with a security device? etc.") The answer was yes.

"Oh, then give me your cards (or your names and addresses), and I'll send you both some information when I get back home."

I did manage to qualify them a bit further as we held the doors open at the next stop. I found out enough about them to decide to send them information and then follow up.

15. Breakfast Clubs

These are the networking clubs that meet at 7:00 a.m., generally once a week. I like mine because when I joined it they told me, "We're strictly a social club. We don't do any community good works. We don't support any charities or sponsor Miss Ramona, or clean horse manure off the streets after the parades. We just have parties."

That attitude was kind of refreshing after all the Good Works I've done in my life. Good Works can become morally heavy when indulged in for too long. I was ready to do some good works for Venus.

Members of networking groups pledge to give each other and send each other business. My particular group was leery of me at first, because they suspected I was one of those Pyramid Multilevelers they had all worked so hard to stay away from. After all, these people were straight-standing members of the business community. It took months, but I gradually wore away their fears. They've come to personally like me since I educated them about multilevel while they ate, drank, and slapped on my samples. I've gotten quite a few retail customers and some distributors from this group. I especially like these distributors because they are already hard working business people who know how to deal with the public.

16. Be A Town Girl (or Guy)

Every afternoon I go to town. In varying order, and on different days, I go to the post office, the bank, the grocery store, the bookstore, the library, the gas station, different restaurants, and the fruit stand. I visit my friends at the interior decorating shop, the jewelry store, and the cleaners. I often sit at one of several outdoor coffee shops and chat with people who drift by on the sidewalks. I look forward to my town visits, and while I'm visiting, I'm always prospecting. I'm building relationships with the many people I see over and over again. I may not mention multilevel for days or weeks, or months, since I wait until the time is right. For example, it took two years and I had to redecorate my house, but June at the interior design shop now says she's ready to join my multilevel.

More Good Advice

I decided long ago that if I wanted to have a good business with good distributors, I had to get out and live.

I couldn't just sit around with my mother and eat peanuts. Frankly, however, I've always believed in hopping into what life offers and squeezing the juice out of each episode. This life-style has caused me lots of emotional excesses, financial losses, and huge windfalls, plus uncountable life experiences. I'm a little worn out, but I'm happy. Here's how I apply my natural way of living to looking for prospects:

Be Observant

I'm observant. I watch people and everything that goes on around me. Because I do that, I often know who to approach and how. I don't miss many opportunities unless I choose to.

For example, awhile back, I was at an airport in New Jersey along with a batch of other anxious people, waiting for a connecting plane to take us to some out of the way place. It was late and dark and everyone was tired and cold. Our particular plane had been grounded. The airline clerks kept saying, "The company is trying to find a plane to replace yours. It should be here soon." It didn't help that small planes kept arriving for everyone else. We waited and waited.

We were a crabby bunch, but most of us managed to hold up our thin coats of civility, except for four men who threw temper tantrums. I curled up in an airport chair and watched the show. First one man, and then another, would race up to the harried young clerks and demand to be put on a plane to our destination *immediately*. One fellow yelled and shook his striped, yellow neck scarf over his head, then flapped it in front of one clerk's face, shouting something about how important he was and how important his meeting was. Then, getting nowhere, he huffed up, raced in a little circle and sat down. Another man, very officious in his long overcoat and soft brown hat, tried another tack. He used charm and supplications. When that didn't work, he lost his veneer of friendliness, showed his teeth, yelled, and banged his briefcase on the floor. The third man ran up to the clerks, shouted a few obscenities, and raced off to the men's room. I liked the forth man best. Each time the airline ladies announced that the next flight could begin boarding, this man would pop up out of his chair like a red-haired giant on springs. It was never our plane. After each hope dashed, the man expressed sharp disappointment. He would shout and shake his fists at heaven, then at his wife for the foolhardiness of the trip. Every plane arrival brought the mandatory outburst that caused him to shoot over to the airline clerks to person-ally express his outrage, alternated with his deep apolo-gies to the women. "I'm sorry. I'm sorry," he'd say con-tritely and sincerely after each tantrum. "I don't mean to lose control." He'd continue, quite reasonably, "Forgive me, I know it's not your fault."

Then, "But God damn it!" he'd scream. "This is out-rageous!" As the night wore on, I noticed his wife had placed herself on the other side of the room.

Being observant, I saw all the screaming fits, of course, but I also noticed a man who also seemed amused by them. It was an easy thing to smile at him and comment on the play around us. With some questioning, I found he was a postal worker who didn't much like his job. Before our plane finally arrived, I had his card, his interest in multi-level, and I had assured him that I'd be in touch, soon, with more information.

Be A Social Being

When I first started multilevel, I was shy. In a classroom setting, I'd never raise my hand because I didn't want to ask a "stupid" question. Outside the classroom, I'd rather have thrown up on my chest than draw attention to myself by speaking to a stranger, or even someone I wasn't comfortable with. Multilevel forced me to peel off my repressions and express myself. I realized that I had to speak up if I wanted to meet people and build a business. Since I was a single mother and desperate, I began talking, but gradually. I said a lot of dumb things and tried many tacks and avenues that didn't work. I practiced, practiced, practiced. Now, I find myself speaking up from an audience and chatting merrily to those mute people that frequent elevators.

No matter how you plan to connect with people, eventually you must start talking. Become social. Join something. Take a group trip to the Salton Sea. Grocery shop everyday. Make yourself say hello to the closest person to you. Think of a compliment to add to it. Nobody will get mad at you for telling them how beautiful their hair is, or asking if they're a radio or TV personality.

A few months ago, I had to spend several days in a booth at a trade show with a woman I didn't know. For some reason, she didn't seem to like me. I was puzzled by this and my feelings were a bit hurt. Midway into the morning she was busily explaining some business facts to me. I was watching her closely and thought, "She is so pretty." Instead of keeping that thought to myself as most of us might, I let the thought become the word. It slid right out of my mouth. The woman stopped short and swung around to look at me as though she wanted to smack me. Unnerved, I said, "Oh. I'm sorry. I didn't mean to offend you. Don't people tell you how pretty you are all the time?" I guess not, because immediately she began fumbling and clacking and cooing, obviously delighted with my observation, once she'd assimilated what I'd said. Her coldness towards me evaporated immediately and before long we were the best of friends. All it had taken to reach her was a simple and true compliment, spoken candidly.

I read somewhere about a man in multilevel who forces himself to socialize at least three times a day by putting three dried kidney beans in his pocket each morning. His goal is to speak to three new people each day about multilevel or his product. Each time he talks to a person, he shifts a bean to another pocket.

No matter how or where you look for distributors, you must learn to talk to them. Practice, practice, practice.

Aside from building a business, your life will be enriched by knowing, even momentarily, a few more people in the multicolored and complex galaxy of human beings. You'll find that meeting new people is like eating rich, nut-studded cake, everyday.

Lucky Is As Lucky Thinks

A lot of people say I'm lucky. I think I'm lucky too, but here's how luck comes to me when I'm looking for good distributors. A few months after I first started my business, I began to spend a lot of time outside lounging in a chaise lounge, looking at the sky. I'd just drift and dream, thinking strongly about how I'd build my multilevel. All kinds of ideas would come to me and I'd write them down on a yellow legal pad. Among other things, I'd picture and feel myself attracting the right kinds of people into my business, seeing them as persistent and dedicated and glad to be with me. I'd get real happy as I did this. I'd lie outside and grin foolishly all day. I had a wonderful time, and oddly, I noticed that after I did this, all kinds of good things would happen. Many more things happened then than had happened during all the weeks and months that I'd spent just recruiting and calling and doing paperwork and worrying. Great people and opportunities (which I took advantage of) just seemed to come to "lucky" me after my long days outside under the sky. Of course, I still had plenty of disappointments and depressions, too. After all, life brings us up to think the worst, and I was reaping the fruit of that seed, daily, along with the more recent flower of good thought.

Even now, every day, I picture money and prosperity raining on me from all good sources. I see the right people coming into my life to join me in my business. I picture and give time to this thought every day, many times a day. I believe wholeheartedly that I'm extremely lucky. And what happens? First, I put myself out in the world so people can find me. I socialize. I do. I also work. Then. . .it happens.

REVIEW
Finding Prospects:
What to Do, Where to Go

1. **Restaurants**
2. **The Beach, the Mall, the Circus, the Grocery Store, Etc.**
3. **Garage Sales**
4. **Barn Sales**
5. **Bake, Estate, and Antique Sales**
6. **Classes and Seminars**

7. Community Work
8. Clubs and Organizations
9. Wrong Numbers and Telephone Solicitors
10. "Solicitors Wanted"
11. Door-to-Door
   • *Cold Calls*
12. Telephone Books and Purchased Mailing Lists
13. Airplanes
14. Elevators
15. Breakfast Clubs
16. Be A Town Girl (or Guy)

And Remeber!
   •Be Observant
   •Be A Social Being
   •Lucky Is As Lucky Thinks

Chapter 4

Advertising for Prospects

It seems like everybody thinks that since they're in multilevel, they've got to advertise. Recently, I signed a lady in another state. I'd never met her, just signed her up over the phone. She called me frantically a few days later. "What'll I do?" she said. "I put an ad in the paper and the phone's ringing like crazy. I've got a couple of ladies coming over today to meet with me about this business. One says she wants to sign up! What'll I do now? I don't know anything about this business."

Advertising is a funny thing. I've found either you don't get any calls or you get too many. When you get a lot, the phone rings all the time, you're constantly talking and explaining and setting up appointments with people and generally running and spinning and feeling like you're getting somewhere quickly. In the end, however, when you look at it, you've often just tossed your time out the window like dandelion seeds blowing in the wind. When the ad runs out and the phone stops ringing, you find that nothing has happened. Nothing has happened but you're shot. Pooped. Worn out and depressed. I did this a few times before I gave it up.

Some people, however, love to advertise and swear by it. If it's your calling, don't let my experience deter you. If you're determined to try it, try it cheap.

The Opportunity Ad

Start with a small ad and put it under the Sales or Business section in the newspaper. (Or, tack it up on a few likely bulletin boards.) Be sure to clearly state what and who you're looking for.

For example: "Looking for people with teaching, sales, or managerial experience, interested in making up to $6,000 a month or more. Call 619-788-0000. Ask for Ms. Deezel."

•State the Type of Person You Want

The reason you state the type of person you want is because you don't want to attract reference librarian or bookkeeper types. You want someone who's probably more outgoing and who knows how to work with people. If you just ask for "people," you'll waste time sorting through the pile.

When you mention $6,000 or whatever, you get people who can think bigger than $950 a month. You won't have to pry their minds open.

When you tell them to ask for a Ms. or Mrs., you're making it easier for them to pick up the phone. People feel more comfortable about calling an unknown woman than they do about calling a man. If you're a man, you can answer the phone saying, "Ms. Deezel is out at the moment, but I can help you." Your voice mail might say, "Ms. Deezel will return your call," then you do it for her.

The ad I've just outlined is called an *Opportunity Ad.*

You're looking for people to join you in the business.

The Product Ad

If you want only retail people for your products, write a *Product Ad*:

"Flagger's White Wonder Powder. Put it on your face and watch the wrinkles suck up the stuff. Puffs your face out so you look fifteen years younger. Call to order. 904-566-0000. Ask for Flossy Flagger."

Handling Calls

Whichever ad you decide to run, give a phone number that feeds into an answering machine, or something similar. Trust me. From my experience, you'll tire fast of answering every call and wading through the folks who aren't interested. After you've recounted your company story fifty times for people who just want to talk or who even try to sell *you* something, you'll switch to an answering device. On the recorder, I strongly advise you to tell the caller what your company is and what your products are. True, you'll lose some who may have a prejudice towards multilevel or your particular company, but better to lose them now than to have to call them and lose them then. People hate it when multilevelers aren't up front with them about their business or opportunity. I have people call and write me all the time who have read my books. Something a lot of them mention is their hatred of going to a distributor's house to find out about a multilevel and having to wait through three hours of multilevel talk before the distributor tells them the company's name or product.*

*For more information on advertising, see *MLM Magic* and the *MLM Magic Workbook*. (1-800-423-0620)

REVIEW
Advertising

1. The Opportunity Ad
  •*State the Type of Person You Want*
2. The Product Ad
3. Handling Calls

Chapter 5

Approaching Prospects

I agree with Achaan Chah who said, "Do everything with a mind that let's go. Do not expect praise or reward." (Or that the person you're talking to will be your retirement!) I approach every person with curiosity and a genuine willingness to like them. I know that most of the time he or she won't be right for my business, but so what. I'll enjoy my momentary (or much longer) connection with the person for whatever it has to offer. There's more to life than money and business.

I prefer to have time to get to know a person. When I finally mention my business or products, it's much more natural. For example, the morning networking breakfast I attend gives me the opportunity to get to know people, and for them to know me. It's the same with classes that meet at least several times and with community organizations that you might join. Recently, I signed Vicky, a lady who works as a secretary for my sister, Polly. Vicky is separated from her husband and needs to make a lot more money than she does. She also seems to like me, is very interested in my products, and over time and with exposure, she has become interested in what I do. Since I see her whenever she is at Polly's office, I simply took my time. Polly kept telling me, "Don't you dare sign her up! She needs to keep her mind strictly on my business!" Well, the day Polly called me and said Vicky was thinking of signing with someone else, I shot over there and gave her a few flyers, some samples, and a little pep talk. It was something like, "Are you going to sign up with me?"

Whether you take days or weeks or two minutes with a prospect, the first thing you need to do is to *interview them*. By interviewing, I mean you need to ask them questions. You need to find out if they're possibly right for multilevel. I ask things like, "What do you do for a living?" or, "Do you like your work?" or, "If you could do anything, what would you do?" (Maybe your MLM will provide them with the money and time to follow that wish.)

1. Begin By Finding Out "Where He/She Is in Life"

You want to find where a person "is" in life so you'll know how to approach him or her. I ask many questions until I get a feel for the person. If they never interject and ask me about myself, I think they're probably not interested in people, and distributors need to be interested in people. I cross lots of folks off my mental list right there. I find out if they have any interest in the kind of products I deal with. You should do the same by asking questions related to your products and business.

2. Be Complimentary

During, or even before the questioning, I *compliment*. Some people in multilevel will tell you to say, "You seem like a really bright person (or good with people, or charismatic, etc.), you'd be perfect for what I do." Then they lead into what they do. Sometimes I do that, if it's the truth. More often, I simply let loose something I find attractive about them. Maybe it's, "You have gorgeous nails. Where do you have them done?" Or, I'll even say to a man, "You have such a neat personality," or whatever. People like to hear nice things about themselves if you mean them. From a compliment, I may jump into my products or business, or I may not. Real compliments may just be part of what warms the conversation.

3. Mention the Product
At some point, *if* the person seems like a potential, I'll *mention my products or business.* I'll find some way, any way, to bring it up. It won't always make sense, but no one seems to notice. Conversations never follow an outline, anyway. They jump around.

4. Give a Sample
If the prospect seems interested, I'll often drag a rumpled sample of something, or a brochure out of my purse. "Oh, look," I'll say with a surprised look on my face, "look what I've got. Here. Take it." Next, I like to quickly pen my name and phone number on the article. I never put slick name stickers on them because it looks premeditated. Or, if I've got the person really excited, I'll say, "Hey. I've got some of that stuff in my car. I was just taking it to a lady, but she can wait. Come on out with me. Let's go get it." I've even signed people up out of my car because I've just "happened to have" a kit or material to sign someone into the business.

When you give your new friend the sample, the brochure, or whatever, say, "*Give me your card. I'll call you to-morrow* and see what you think of the stuff." Never just give them your card and say, "Call me if you like it." I think there are landfills especially for business cards. People get home with those expensive little wonders and toss them. Few people actually save and use them. You, my darling, must recontact your prospect.

"But, Venus, give me more detail. How do I talk to prospects?" All you need to remember is this: Change that word *to* to *with*. Most people in multilevel tend to attack a person, using the talking *to* approach. We pin a person to the ground and start telling them everything they don't want to know about our products and business. A much more effective approach is to talk *with* them. Most of the scenarios I've already told you about illustrate this approach. Asking your prospects questions about themselves and their lives and listening to the information creates a two-way conversation, not a one-way conversation run by a strident zealot.

Preventing Disastrous Approaches

My, my. I bet all of you could write your own book on all your disastrous approaches. I could. Remember the old couple that hotly resented my telling them they'd been in the wrong multilevel for all those years? And, if you've read *MLM Magic*, you remember the disastrous Christmas dinner with Fanny's cousin that cured me forever of attacking prospects.

1. Stop and Think
Before you approach someone and before you open

your mouth, stop a moment and think, "Would I want someone trying to drag me into their multilevel?" I bet you wouldn't. Awhile back, I told you the story about my brother Jim who worked as a waiter at the restaurant where masses of multilevel people socialized and cruised for prospects. Jim wanted me to go there just to watch them in action. I was vociferous about saying "No!" The idea of being approached and verbally raked by rabid distributors made the skin on my body stiffen and shriek.

2. Don't Hustle or Harass

A few years ago I was on an airplane, returning to California from Hawaii. I was with a group of multilevel people, including an old couple sitting next to me, Edith and Charlie. I hoped to get a little relaxation and a snooze, but that was not to be. The old couple were devout trollers for prospects. This meant they were always looking, always talking, and always trying. They seemed to give no thought to the suitability or interest of those they hustled and harassed. We were seated in the middle section of the plane which gave them a wide range. They began by accosting the people in the seats in front of them, the seats behind them, the seats to the left, and finally, to me, on their far right. I was quite amazed. There were no preliminaries. They had a simple approach. "We're involved with this wonderful company, here's a brochure, would you like to make $5,000 a month? We have great products, we're sure you can fit it around your job and your family—look, you'll never get anywhere with what you're doing now. Let us show you all the numbers, hmm?" For a couple of hours they drew intricate marketing plans, raved about their super products, plied people with flyers, and harangued passersby who had no thought except making it to the bathroom. Finally, finding no response, they settled their attentions on one harried redhaired stewardess. The poor woman couldn't pass a cup of tea without being regaled with the marvels of the couple's multilevel. The stewardess had brochures and flyers stuffed in her pockets, samples of products slipped into her hands, testimonials called after her as she served chicken pie, and amazing numbers drawn out for her on cocktail napkins. I was exhausted. During a break in the attack, I tried to nap a bit. Moments later, however, there was a frenzied whispering to my left. I opened one eye. Our stewardess was leaning over the old couple, speaking animatedly, but quietly, with a little bundle of something clutched in her hands.

"You've really got to try it," she insisted as she looked quickly over her shoulder. "I do this on the side when I'm not flying. They're wonderful products and you can't beat the marketing plan!" I opened both eyes and snorted a bit. I looked intently at the old couple. I didn't want to miss this. One of their victims had turned on them! Now they'd see what it was like. "Here," Cheri the stewardess said dramatically, "rub this perfume on your wrist. Isn't it grand? It's a copy of a famous one from Paris. And, here, try this one." From her pocket she produced a purple bottle, aimed it at Charlie and sprayed. I could see that he enjoyed it. In fact, both he and Edith were speechless. "Now," Cheri said as she hunkered down in the aisle, "let me tell you the history of this stuff and this company, and then I'll show you the marketing plan."

"Well, I don't think," Charlie said, "that we'd be. . . ."

"Oh wait!" Cheri announced. "Here, try this scent." Out of her pocket appeared a small red atomizer. Charlie winced and choked as he was sprayed again.

"Jasmine," Cheri stated. "Don't you just love it?"

Without waiting for an answer, Cheri proceeded to make good on her promise to educate Charlie and Edith about the entire history of the company, the products, and the marketing plan. Periodically, she was called to her regular duties, but she always returned to the old couple, clutching a new brochure, flyer, or atomizer bottle. Charlie was beginning to smell like the perfume section of a five and dime. Protestations did no good. No matter what Charlie or Edith said about having no interest or time or money to sign with Cheri and her company, it didn't deter Cheri. She always had a comeback. At one point she even leaned across them and propositioned me. I said, "No thank you. I have a business and I don't want another one." This didn't stop Cheri. When she found I had a daughter, she said, "Well, that's it then. Your daughter will sell these products. What's her name and phone number?"

The rest of the trip found Charlie and Edith quite subdued. They were never able to relax, watch the movie, or even go to the bathroom without Cheri popping up and hovering beside them. I smiled like a big happy cat and went to sleep. The universe does work perfectly. What goes around comes around.

REVIEW
Approaching Prospects

1. **Begin By Finding Out "Where He/She Is in Life"**
2. **Be Complimentary**
3. **Mention the Product**
4. **Give a Sample**

Preventing Disastrous Approaches
1. Stop and Think
2. Don't Hustle or Harass

Chapter 6

A Few Days in the Life of a Prospector (What You Can Learn From Others' Experiences)

Jim & Hugh

Just for fun, and to help you feel better about your prospecting attempts, let's review several days of prospecting by my brother Jim and my friend Hugh. After telling me and all the different distributors at the restaurant where he worked that he'd never, ever sign up in a multi-level, Jim finally did. Briefly. Under Hugh. They tried working as a team, selling a diet product called *Fat Off* and a Miracle Vitamin Cookie. Here are a few days in their lives. . .see what you can learn from them.

If You're Selling It, You've Got to Eat (Use, Wear, etc.) It

Jim knows everyone. He's what I call a Bird Dog. He'll point people out, and Hugh is expected to run and bag them. Recently, he gave Hugh six names of people he guaranteed would be frothing with anticipation while waiting for Hugh's call. Hugh dutifully contacted them. The people weren't waiting and they weren't frothing. In fact, they never returned Hugh's calls. I guess they only resonated to Jim. Or, Jim thought they did.

Jim said not to worry about it, that he was bringing a hot prospect over for Hugh to meet and sign today.

Now, I must let you know that Jim has been doing something wrong. He is using his Fat Off, but he isn't eating his company's Miracle Vitamin Cookie. "Tastes like dry weeds laced with bed bugs," he said.

"It doesn't matter," I told him. "If you're selling it, you've got to eat it!"

Jim brings over Dirk to meet with Hugh. Dirk, it turns out, is twenty-two years old and an ex-Calvin Klein model. His butt is the size of a football and just as tight. With every hair greased in place, his body tanned to Thanksgiving turkey color, he's wearing slim Calvin Klein jeans and is waiting to be shown the Million Dollar Diet Business.

Shortly, Jim is wowing Dirk with the fat monitoring machine and the Fat Off products, and how far you can go with the company, and how much money they're all gonna' make—and doesn't Fat Off taste spectacular? Jim and Hugh and Dirk can actually hear all that money jangling up and down in their pant's pockets.

Presently, Hugh clears his throat a bit and speaks up. "Have you tried the Miracle Vitamin Cookie, yet?" he asks. Jim rolls his eyes and looks hugely annoyed. "Ah geez," he says. He knows Dirk is much too citified, too sophisticated and worldly to want to eat old weeds and ground bedbugs. Dirk looks at Hugh and says, "What's that?"

Within two minutes Dirk has chewed and swallowed

the Miracle and is raving, "I love it. I love it. I tell you, I feel something! I feel high. I feel like I've been eating weed, man! Weed! What's in this stuff? Give me another one!"

Jim can't believe it.

They spend three hours with Dirk, feeding him Miracle Vitamin Cookies and the marketing plan. Dirk no longer cares about the Fat Off. He wheedles a free box of Miracle Cookies off the boys and gets them to give him a break and promise to sell him a case of the Cookies at their cost as soon as he can get the money for it. He doesn't sign up as a distributor because he has to get the money for that, too. One last cookie, and he's out the door, never, as it turns out, to be seen again.

Several days after the Dirk incident, Hugh has a list of people who need to be contacted. He's roaring to go. To date he's got one lady taking the Fat Off products. She's got terrible gas from the diet, but she's so fat they hope maybe she'll manage to just blow some of the fat off.

First off, Hugh and I go to the local Tractor Cap Restaurant for breakfast. I'm helping him out since Jim has other business today. Hugh and I are here because a few days ago he left some diet samples with the hefty waitress, Saviola, when she had begged him for the Fat Off. Today she tells Hugh she gave the stuff to her brother-in-law who came up from Texas. She did it because she doesn't need those samples now, she hopes Hugh doesn't mind. She's on a fabulous diet that lets you eat all the carbohydrates you want, once a day. She then looks heavenward and describes the huge black brownie with the one inch thick chocolate frosting that she ate late last night after three plates of fat spaghetti with Parmesan cheese and chunky tomato sauce. And today she's having deep-dish pizza with pecan ice cream and maybe a slab of yellow cake with more of that rich chocolate frosting she likes so much.

I wish her luck as she waddles off and I turn to Hugh and say, "Let's go to the mall." Hugh's ready. He looks kind of sad and depressed.

Stay Alert for the Unexpected

We go and wear ourselves out window shopping. I keep telling Hugh, "Relax. You just need to meet more people. You never know where you'll find the right people for your business."

While flat tuckered out, sitting on a bench, and drinking cappuccino, a seventy year old lady sits down across from us and starts chatting. She tells us about her knee replacement and how she now golfs and swims but how she really needs to lose the weight she put on while she was laid up. I give Hugh a little kick. He says, "Have you heard of Fat Off?" She hasn't, but she wants to. It turns out that Flo lives in the wealthiest town in our county, has a large circle of fat friends, and begs Hugh, just begs him, to come and give a Fat Off talk to the ladies in her club. "The ladies will just go crazy over you," she says, looking at his dimples. "Bring your fat machine and all your stuff."

Later, as we dance our way to the car, I say to Hugh, "You know, I think that meeting people like this, accidentally, is potentially lots more profitable than any type of advertising or trying to convince regular people that they need to lose weight or join a multilevel."

Remember, What Goes Down Must Come Up

As for Hugh's next appointment that afternoon at a spa, we found when we arrived that the spa manager had gone home for the day, and the secretary told us she had just called Hugh's house to cancel the appointment.

You'll find your days, weeks, months, and even years of multilevel are like this. Up and down. Up and down. Your prospecting attempts will lurch from grief and huge disappointment to great hopes and happiness. Just remember, when you're up, you gotta' come down, and when you're down, you'll always move back up. To simplify matters and save yourself from either a heart attack or quitting, consider emotionally leveling out. When things go poorly, it's okay, and when things go splendidly, that's okay too.

REVIEW
What You Can Learn
From Others' Experiences

1. If You're Selling It, You've Got to Eat (Use, Wear, etc.) It
2. Stay Alert for the Unexpected
3. Remember, What Goes Down Must Come Up

CHAPTER 7

FOLLOW UP

Let's say you've found and approached someone in a tactful way. You've gotten their interest and given them a sample or brochure. You've gotten their name and number but you weren't able to give them a presentation right there or make an appointment to see them in person in a day or two. You've told them that you'll call the next day and see if they liked the sample or see what they thought of the brochure. Or, you told them you'd send them something. Or, you've had a response on an ad you've placed. Now what? You need to recontact the prospect.

You Must Recontact Your Prospect

Let's talk about that. Reconnecting is called follow-up. We all know it's hard, in the beginning, to make that first contact with someone. We also know that it generally takes a lot of practice to do it with ease and confidence. Surely, then, most of us think that once we've finally managed to connect with someone we'd follow up.

Ha. I'd say that nine out of ten of us won't attempt to harvest the grain we've so laboriously sown. Why not? I think we get cold chicken feet, that's what I think. We've done all this work, thoroughly scared ourselves to death by approaching people, felt elated that we finally did, and then, somehow, we don't do the next step. Actually, there are many reasons why we slack off, not just that we've got Chickenitis.

Sometimes distributors don't ask a prospect for their name and phone number. They just give the person their card and expect the prospect to phone them ready to sign up. As I mentioned earlier, the prospect won't call, and you just wasted your time, since you don't have a phone number or address or any way of reaching them.

Stay Alert for Sabotage

Sometimes while you've been working on a prospect, a member of your family or a friend will at that moment, or later, cut you down in front of them. Sofie, a distributor of mine, has a sister and a brother-in-law, Don the Doctor, who, when he has the chance, will assure Sofie's prospects that there are no proven medical claims for Sofie's herbal and vitamin wonders. Another woman's father will intone, "It's a scam. I know Robin's doing great with the company, but it won't last. Mark my word." After these kinds of testimonials from your closest supporters, follow-up feels rather pointless.

Is Your Prospect Defensive?
Be Smart and Back Off

Maybe your prospect says, "Yeah, well it looks good, but it's too expensive. I've heard it doesn't muscle test well, I'm burnt out on MLM, the FDA probably doesn't like it,

I'll need to check with the Better Business Bureau, and I don't know if I want to try the stuff. But, hey, call me with more information." Your subconscious mind, at least, if not your conscious mind says, "I'm not calling this woman back!"

Don't Let the Days Slip By

Sometimes, the days get away from a person and pretty soon you realize you sent a sample out to Mr. Wheezer two or three weeks ago, and gosh, he's probably forgotten all about it. And you want to too.

Sometimes your dysfunctional self gets in the way. Once, I was busily prospecting a woman who was opening a large health food store. She was anxious to sign up with me and make my products available. One Sunday she called about 7:30 a.m. and said, "I'm ready to talk seriously about this. I want to chug up the mountain to your house right now and meet with you."

I was still in bed. I'd been fighting for five days with my boyfriend of five years and it was the terminal point in our relationship. We had just reached the decision to stop seeing each other. I said to the woman, "I can't. I just can't today."

That day led into several weeks and then several months. Once I'd come up from the bottom of my emotional ocean, I'd called the woman but could never reach her. I did find her, though, two months later at a company meeting where she was being pinned as a supervisor. . .under someone else. I had done lousy follow-up.

I'm also guilty of not calling soon enough after I meet people, and I've also given up on people before I should have. I only know that for sure when I find the person signed up with someone else at a meeting or hear they've signed into another multilevel.

And you should see the audios, videos, and mail I get, unsolicited, from people who never contact me again. That kind of behavior is a clear example of no follow-up, and that has to equal no sign-ups for these people too. Maybe these folks forget they send me stuff, or maybe the phone just gets too heavy to lift.

Watch Out for the Heavy Phone Syndrome

The Heavy Phone Syndrome is common. It's associated with Chickenitis. The only way to recover from that disease is to make yourself pick up the phone, dial, and start talking. And, do it over and over again. Whenever I have to do something like this that scares me I think, "I'm just practicing." Each time I bungle a call or a contact I think, "Well. That didn't work! But, I was just practicing." Then, I practice some more.

You must follow-up. Follow-up and follow-up until you either sign the prospect or until they tell you plainly that they have absolutely no interest. Then you can lay off, but you still may want to occasionally mail them a note or a newsletter, or something else that's unobtrusive.

And, sorry, but even after you've signed someone up, you still have to follow-up to make sure they get trained.

REVIEW
Follow Up

1. **You Must Recontact Your Prospect**
2. **Stay Alert for Sabotage**
3. **Is Your Prospect Defensive?**
   Be Smart and Back Off
4. **Don't Let the Days Slip By**
5. **Watch Out for the Heavy Phone Syndrome**

CHAPTER 8

SETTING APPOINTMENTS, PRESENTING YOUR OPPORTUNITY, AND SIGNING DISTRIBUTORS

One-On-Ones

If you've read my books, *MLM Magic* and the *MLM Magic Workbook*, you know in detail how I meet someone, present my business to them, and sign them up. My way is different from the way other experienced distributors teach, because I don't like to set up and do what are called *one-on-ones*. I like to sign people where I find 'em.

If you want to set an appointment for a one-on-one, however, you might say to a prospect, "Hey, let's get together tomorrow or Tuesday for coffee. Is two o'clock good, or would three be better?" Or even, "Do you have about fifteen minutes? Let's step over here and I'll go over this plan with you."

One-on-ones make me nervous. Generally, people use company presentation folders with these. A person giving a one-on-one will sit you down and *slowly* flip those darn pages in their *huge* three ring binder that outlines their company's very beginnings right up to the present, replete with laminated graphs and charts and six pages of the wowzer marketing plan. It's an enormous bore. I also dread these appointments because unless you set them up at their home, your prospects are quite likely not going to show up. But, hey, you can set appointments if you want to. Maybe you'll be good at it. Do what feels right for you.

Opportunity of the Moment

As I said, I prefer to *present the opportunity at the moment I meet a person,* or *over the phone later.* Sometimes I do it after I've met with them a number of times when they didn't have a clue about my future intent. That would be someone I'd come to know through a class or church or similar. Whatever you decide, here's an example of my basic approach:

In my morning networking group, I met a lady named Marvel. She invited me to stop by her place sometime and see her doll collection. "Don't bother to call," she said, "if you see my car, just come on over."

So I did. With something in mind other than dolls.

Marvel and I chatted for awhile about her dolls and her life. Then I gave her a *sincere compliment.* "You'd be really good at my business," I said. "You have a lot of charm and connect well with people."

Next I spent about *five minutes* very casually telling her about my *company and products.* No charts, no graphs, no three ring binders. I didn't even show her a brochure. "If it sounds interesting to you," I said, "it's easy enough to make money." I then gave her a *very simple marketing plan* explanation. I left out all the fancy stuff about how to make bonuses and how many cases would add up to Hawaii and how many levels you needed to conquer China.

Closing

Then, I *closed* her. I said, "I needed to change my life and I did it with this. Would you like to do what I did?" When Marvel said, "Well, maybe. . ." I whipped out an *application,* plunked it down on the table, and said, "It's $42 and all you have to do is sign here. What do you want to do?"

Marvel signed. They don't always. That just means they aren't interested and you'll find someone else, or you need to spend more time with this person, either now or later.

Practice

Constant practice will make you very good at this casual technique. You'll become so deft you'll find yourself signing people in movie lines, parking lots, and while you're shopping. Then, of course, you'll have to ask yourself if you want all these distributors!

REVIEW

Setting Appointments, Presenting Your Opportunity, and Signing Distributors

1. One-On-Ones
2. Opportunity of the Moment
3. Closing
4. Practice

CHAPTER 9

HOW TO KNOW WHO TO HELP
AND WHO TO LET GO

Now you have a raft of distributors. Or maybe just one or two. You think you're set for life, that your retirement is just up the street, that your golden horse will win the derby. Then you notice something. No one is *doing* anything. Some of your distributors keep assuring you that they will. Others hop up and down and shout that they're going to make you rich. Others say they'll build this business, they surely will, as soon as they get their husband straightened out, their kids off to college, the boss stops picking on them at their real job, they get back from all their Halloween parties, as soon as Uncle Fudley gets into the rest home, and as soon as the sun drops out of the sky. They're gonna' build this business as soon as they learn everything about it, as soon as they're sure this really isn't a pyramid scheme, as soon as their wife decides to emotionally back them, and as soon as they pull together enough money to buy some product.

From other distributors you'll hear only silence. They won't be home when you call, and they'll forget all your meetings or have emergency dental appointments or frontal lobotomies scheduled on those evenings. Other distributors will just piddle along and give you hope. Some will screech into the business, peak sharply, and disappear. A very few will actually do something and be steady about it.

Who should you help and spend your time with? The answer seems simple. Spend your time with those who do things and not with those who don't. The problem is, how can you know who's what, especially with so many folks hopping around and promising huge output, while others are quietly going to sleep or silently shoveling out the foundation for a solid business? Sometimes it's impossible to know who will persist and actually build a viable multilevel. Here are a few ways to try to distinguish true business builders from all the rest.

Notice Who Calls You

A man named Hooter says, "Stop dragging your distributors down the road. Ask them to follow you. Notice if they call you. Notice if they purchase product, go to meetings, read your newsletters, and ask your advice. Do you see or hear a lot from them? If not, they probably aren't serious."

I think Hooter is probably right. He also has said to me, "I never call my downline. They have to call me. Then I know they're serious."

I think he has a point, but it's stretched a bit far for my taste. I do call my downline. But, if they don't call me back, and/or never call me, I take that as a sign that their interest is evaporating. I do, however, get newsletters to my downline once a month and attempt to let them know about the latest meetings and conference calls. I've had people tell me, "I'd never have stuck with you for six years, except for those newsletters."

Begin Noticing Personal Patterns

There's something else I've noticed about distributors. They each have a personal pattern they follow. For example, I have a man who could be a silver studded star in MLM. Unfortunately for both of us, his light bulbs only come on periodically. He'll start snorting huge gulps of multilevel air while he seriously tells me he's building the biggest business I ever saw! He's hot now, he says, and he's getting ready to sign up half of his state and next the world. He turns into a frenzied, glittering gizmo, typing up newsletters and mailing them, calling each of his downline several times a week and figuring out how he'll be able to retire in two years. I'll hear from him almost everyday for a month or two and then he's gone. Just vaporized, lost in the foggy mists, somewhere on the west coast of California. Then, six months later, I'll hear from him again, and the entire act will be repeated with the same embellishments and flourishes. Six months later he'll come around again. And again. It's his pattern. I stopped getting excited about his potential quite some time ago.

Then there's Denise. She'll bump along getting two cases of product a month, then nothing for six months. Then she's back to two.

And Trudee. She was going to cover the country with her business. As she's said many times, "I can do whatever I put my mind to. I can make a huge go of this. I'm going to do it, too. After I finish my schooling. . .after I get my real estate license. . .after I get married . . .I'm really gonna' do it, now." I've been hearing this for five years.

Start noticing the patterns your distributors develop.

You'll be able to count on this being the way they'll always operate. When you see that Riley always calls you several times a day with questions, but never orders any product, you'll know that he'll probably never order any and so you don't need to spend too much, or any time, with him. You'll stop getting revved up and hopeful when Orida, who owned the biggest real estate company in Tennessee, tells you for the twenty-third time in a year, "Just you wait, I'm going to build a whopping business. I've done it before and I have all the contacts." You'll stop getting stirred up because finally you'll notice that she always says this, but that in a year she only has one distributor who orders one case of pressed peanut juice every six months, while Orida herself orders less.

Let Time Be the Judge

Ultimately, time will show you which distributors to work with and which to let go. Before time shows that, however, give your people every opportunity and offer every help.

REVIEW

How to Know Who To Help and Who To Let Go

1. Notice Who Calls You
2. Begin Noticing Personal Patterns
3. Let Time Be the Judge

CHAPTER 10

SUMMING UP

This is the end of my prospecting suggestions but not the end for you. Don't make the mistake so many of us have made which is to finally sign someone, gasp "Thank God!" hand them some stuff, tell them what to do, and run off looking for the next person. You must train your babies. This means you must teach them everything you've learned about how to prospect and sign people, how to overcome slumps and depressions, how to sell your products, and how to give and go to meetings.

Prospecting and signing a distributor is a lot like dating and getting married. It's often a darn hard and upsetting business, but when you finally meet the One, capture their heart, and get them signed up for life with you, the work really starts.

My final suggestion is that when prospecting, as when building your entire business, persist, persist, and persist. As Winston Churchill said, "Never, never, never, never give up." Things will often look bad and you may be depressed more often than you are elated. Multilevel is fraught with crisis and uncertainty, but for many of those people *who stay* comes early retirement, the extra $500 to $1,000 to $50,000 or more a month, the fortune, the increased social life, and/or the giant nest egg and the satisfaction of having won an economic battle.

When you're tempted to say, "That's it, I've prospected hundreds of people and have no one of consequence," or, "Eula would be perfect for this business, but she ignores my every attempt so I'm never gonna' call her, again," reflect on the following story.

Bert decided that Ramzel and his wife Elise would love his business. He'd studied them and realized that they had all the qualifications needed to become successful distributors. He also determined that they were the ones who could make him the most money. He gave them a call, "Say what, I've got this great deal here. I'm gonna' send you some information," he shouted. The chosen couple made little comment. Bert reflected on the matter a bit and thought, "What the heck. They're gonna' love this deal. I'll just send 'em a sign-up kit!" Which he did. When Ramzel and Elise received it, they made a collective face and stuffed it under their bed.

Bert waited awhile for their excited call of acceptance. It didn't come. Finally, he called them. "What'd ya' think?" he asked. "Don't it seem like the finest deal you ever heard of?"

Ramzel and Elise were silent.

"Just read it over," Bert suggested gamely.

Ramzel and Elise pulled the kit out from under the bed and mailed it back. When Bert received it, he thought, "I wonder if this means they don't want to do the business?"

He invited them for dinner. Ramzel told his wife,

"We'll go, but we won't talk about that damn multilevel."

The dinner was good. Bert talked about his terrific multilevel. Ramzel and Elise said nothing.

When the couple returned home, Bert said, "Don't talk to me about that multilevel. I don't ever want to hear about it, again."

Elise agreed, saying, "That Bert is going to drive us crazy."

She was right. Bert was persistent. He knew, deep in his heart that Ramzel and Elise, once they understood the concept, would love his business. For awhile, he called them every other day. When they started to seem a bit abrupt with him, a little short, he sat down and rethought his approach. "Maybe," he thought, "if I push 'em too hard, they'll never listen to me." He took a different tack. Once a month he quietly mailed them his company's journal. "You never know," he reasoned, "someday when they're bored, they might open one, or at a moment when Ramzel's depressed with his job he'll glance over at the journal and wonder what's inside it."

Next, he began sending a copy of his upline's check. When his check started to look like something, he sent that, too. Every once and again, he'd mail them a sample of one of his products. Occasionally he'd give them a cheery call and a giggle, "Gettin' my stuff?" he'd boom. "Not driving you crazy am I?"

One night Elise woke up at two a.m. "Ramzel," she said, giving him a little shove to wake him. "I've been thinking. I want to do that business."

Ramzel was less than supportive.

"I'm serious," Elise said as she rolled out of bed. "I'm ready to get started, right now."

She went to the phone and called Bert. She figured he

deserved a call at two a.m. for all the times he'd harassed them. She was also certain that Bert would be excited to hear from her, no matter what the time, since she was finally accepting his offer. She was right. Bert hopped out of bed and was ready to come right over and start training her.

Ramzel was disgusted. However, after six months passed and Elise began making some good money, he said, "Darling, I think you need my help with this business."

Today, Ramzel and Elise are the top earners in Bert's downline. Bert still prospects everyday. He hits the same stubborn walls he did before and talks and talks and talks to people who couldn't give a jangle about his opportunity. Every once in awhile he signs someone up who does a little something. He's looking for more of those and for another Ramzel and Elise. He's learned the magic method: Never, never, never give up. Persist, persist, persist.

Those last two sentences sum up prospecting and actually, the business of building a multilevel as well. Find a company that's right for you and never give it up. Eventually, we'll see each other at the head of the networking parade.

Wishing you much success and a happy journey.

Love,

     Venus

To contact Venus, send a stamped,
self-addressed envelope to:
Venus Andrecht
c/o Ransom Hill Press
PO Box 325
Ramona, CA 92065

$\mathcal{R}$ansom $\mathcal{H}$ill $\mathcal{P}$ress

PO Box 325 Ramona, CA 92065
(800) 423-0620 • Canada & Outside US (760) 789-0620
• FAX (760) 789-1582 •

Other Titles by Venus Andrecht

Item #MLM	MLM Magic	$16.95
Item #SM	MLM Magic (Spanish version)	$18.95
Item #WB	MLM Magic Workbook	$18.95
Item #PR	Prospecting	$12.95
Item #BB	Bad Blues	$13.95
Item #NB	The Herb Lady's Notebook	$16.95
Item #(ANY)	Postcards: 1 style/set of 30	$7.00
Item #PC-MIX	Postcards: Mixed set of 99/11 ea. style	$19.95
Item #TS-CAT	T-shirt "In MLM, you can choose your office companions"	
Item #TS-OFF	T-shirt "A Networker's Summer Office"	M/L/XL $16.00
		XXL $18.00
		XXXL..$19.00

Volume Discounts on Two or More Items
CALL FOR A *FREE* CATALOG!